The
Church
in the
House
a Return to Simplicity

Robert Fitts

PREPARING THE WAY Publishers

"Making ready a people for the Lord."
Luke 1:17

2121 Barnes Avenue SE
Salem, OR 97306 USA

First Printing, April 2001

Published by

2121 Barnes Avenue SE
Salem, OR 97306 USA

ISBN 1-929451-07-5
Library of Congress Catalog Card Number 2001-130305

Printed in the United States of America

Foreword

Dear Brother Bob,

Your article on house churches was excellent. It reflects what many of us have believed for years, that the expansion of the gospel to all the nations would require a simple, infinitely reproducible form of church planting. This is the kind of church planting that is found in the Scriptures itself, as well as in countries like China, Burma, and Nepal, where open worship and witness is not permitted.

In our denomination, our most rapidly growing works in restricted-access nations are house church movements. In Sri Lanka, Nepal, Pakistan, and Burma this is true. Further, in other countries where there is a measure of freedom, house churches are also being encouraged as the quickest way to get a true movement happening. The biggest challenge in opening minds to house churches is in countries where the gospel has been present for many years, like in European and Latin American countries. Asia has proven the easiest to encourage house churches.

Bob, I would entreat you to wisely and sensitively encourage house churches wherever you go, especially in third-world countries. Also, help the people stay humble about it all, lest they look down on believers who have and believe in buildings. Help people to lovingly make room for different methodologies — that is what we are really talking about. What is important is that we get the gospel to the whole world as quickly and as effectively as possible. In some cases, buildings may be needed, in many other cases house churches will work and, in a few places, perhaps both will be needed. If the fulfillment of the Great Commission is our goal, then let's use any legitimate means available to get the job done. I believe there is no more effective way to fulfill this goal than planting new churches, and house churches are some of the most efficient types we can plant.

In Jesus' bonds,

John Amstutz, *Bible College and Seminary Professor*

Contents

Introduction

In the summer of 1969 I began to pray that God would give me disciples in every country. At the time there were about 220 countries total. Four years earlier God had impressed upon me to pray for each country by name, giving me the promise of Psalm 2:8, *"Ask of me and I will give you the nations for your inheritance and the uttermost parts of the earth for your possession."* From that time it was a joy to pray and believe that the Lord was going to do something to enable me to touch every country for Him.

My plan at the time was to multiply disciples by concentrating on one person and then teaching him to do the same. That way, in time, we would see disciples in every country by the process of multiplication through prayer, faith, and patience. With that in mind, I began to pray more fervently. As I have prayed and moved toward the vision over the years, the Lord has revealed that the best way to multiply disciples is to multiply churches, small groups of disciples.

I sincerely believe that it was in answer to this prayer that the Lord began to change my life and my circumstances so that I went through a very long and difficult period of preparation. As the years went by, I was tempted to lay aside the vision as being just a wild dream filled with personal ambition that had not come from the Lord at all. But somehow I could not let it die within me.

On a quiet afternoon in the fall of 1990, I was on my knees in my bedroom in the city of Riverside, California. During this prayer time, I was reading *Mission Frontiers*, a periodical put out by the United States Center for World Mission, which was founded by Dr. Ralph Winter. The article I was reading was about a mighty move of God in China. I kept coming across the phrase *house church movement*. Suddenly a flash of revelation exploded within my spirit. I can almost say that I felt it physically. "House Churches!" I was not shouting, but my spirit was. "Yes! That's it! I can plant house churches! Praise the Lord! I know I can start churches in houses!" My excitement knew no bounds.

I had been walking through a long, dry desert spiritually. I had laid down everything. I had been stripped of ministry, house, airplane, health — even hope was dying within me. I felt that somehow I had not responded to the Lord in the right ways over the years and that I would never see the fulfillment of the vision of disciples in all nations. Then when that simple little idea of house churches was introduced to me through what was happening in China, a new birth of vision began to rise within me.

I arose from my knees and began to walk and think, pray and plan. "Now I know that I can plant churches — lots of churches!" My spirit soared. My faith was restored. For more than twenty years I had majored in house groups. For five of those years I had helped form hundreds of house groups for children's evangelism. For four years I had been pastor of a house church myself. I knew, firsthand, their many advantages.

For years I had known that the most rapid growth of the Church took place in the first two centuries of the Christian Movement. Now I was reading about the phenomenal growth that was taking place in China — through a House Church Movement. As these two thoughts came together in my mind, the explosion occurred. I could not escape the obvious conclusion: the most dramatic Church growth in history, both in ancient times and in modern times, occurred where there were no church buildings.

Not long after this, I did a study in the New Testament on *the church in the house,* and wrote an eight-page paper entitled "The Case For House Churches." I began to share it with others and found that people were interested. In some places there was red-hot interest. I went to Mexico not long after I wrote the paper, and it was translated into Spanish.

As the Lord opened my understanding to what was in the New Testament and Church history about the *church that meets in the house,* and as I had more and more contact with

8

others who had seen the vision for simple church, I began to write more on the subject, adding to the eight-page paper, calling it "Saturation Church Planting." It fell into the hands of various church leaders and, over a period of four years, was sent out to about forty countries. I began to receive letters from church leaders in many countries asking for more information on the *church that meets in the house*. The following is an effort to share what the Lord has been teaching us over the past ten years about going back to SIMPLE CHURCH.

Throughout the following pages, I have sought to keep before me the wise counsel of Dr. John Amstutz, a long-time friend and a leading mission strategist and teacher to the Body of Christ. Several months ago I sent him a copy of the paper "The Case For House Churches," and he wrote me a valuable commentary on it. I have included it as the Foreword of this book.

ONE

Mission Statement

The church that meets in the house of Charles and Linda, 1492 Palmyrita in Riverside, California, at 7 p.m. every Tuesday, is a community church. We have open meetings with everyone participating, singing praises to Jesus and seeking to build up one another in love. Everyone is important. We read the Bible together and discuss it in an informal way. Anyone wanting to participate joins in the reading and the discussion. All things are done for encouragement.

The group prays for each other, for other churches, for families, relatives, friends, and neighbors; we pray for our president and our country. We minister to one another through prayer, prophetic words, the gifts of the Spirit, and through material aid as the Lord leads. They often have a meal together and celebrate the Lord's Supper.

There is no membership list. Those who belong to the Lord are all members one of another. All seek to follow the instructions about how to meet given by the Apostle Paul in 1 Corinthians 14:26:

> When you come together everyone has a hymn, or a
> word of instruction, a revelation, a tongue or an

interpretation. All of these must be done for the strengthening of the church.

We believe that God's provision for church leadership is through self-supporting elders trained right in the local church as servant leaders. We love one another, are fully accountable to one another, help one another, and are willing to pour out our lives for each other.

The Church is a people — not a building, an organization, a business, or an institution. We are the people of God through faith in the Lord Jesus Christ Who died on the cross to pay for our sins.

When we grow too large for the space we have, our plan is to start another church in another house. The church that meets at Charles's and Linda's was "born pregnant." It was born with a vision to give birth to another church. We fully expect that every church birthed out of this one will also be "born pregnant."

We have a deep desire to see the Bride of Christ grow in purity and effectiveness. We make no claim to perfection, but we are learning — and sharing as we learn; and we are asking some difficult questions. We need your prayers and your kind input as we follow the leading of our Lord Jesus Christ.

We seek to relate to the whole body of Christ within our locality and not just to those who attend our fellowship. Since we are all members of one another, we encourage all that come to this gathering to attend other meetings of the body of Christ as the Holy Spirit directs. We are submitted to spiritual authority wherever it crosses our path. We do not believe in "selective submission," which says in essence, "I am submitted to this group or that leader and to no other."

All the "one another" verses in the writings of Paul were addressed to the city-wide church and not to a local congregation, therefore we submit to all the saints and all the elders within the city-wide church. We are responsible to God and to one another to fulfill all our commitments with regard to service within the Body of Christ.

Saturation church planting is a vision to form churches everywhere for the purpose of fulfilling the Great Commission through evangelism, discipleship, and world missions. The house church is an effective tool to evangelize and disciple the city, and a vehicle to reach out to all nations. We invite you to "come over and help us."

TWO

The Case for House Churches

> Greet Priscilla and Aquila, my fellow workers in Christ Jesus. Greet also the church that meets at their house (Romans 16:3).

> The churches in the province of Asia send you greetings. Aquila and Priscilla greet you warmly in the Lord, and so does the church that meets at their house (1 Corinthians 16:19).

> Give my greetings to the brothers at Laodicea, and to Nympha and the church in her house (Colossians 4:15).

> To Philemon, our dear friend and to the church that meets in your home (Philemon 1-2).

From the above Scriptures it is clear that the early Church met in homes. They did not have church buildings. Such buildings did not appear until the year A.D. 232. In those early days they were not called *house churches*. Instead, they were called *the Church* that met in the house of someone. It is notable that the most explosive period of Church growth in history, until recently, took place during those early years.

However, right now in China, there is an unprecedented movement that even surpasses that early growth of the Church. This unparalleled revival is a house church movement. The following is taken from the "Caleb Report" in the 1990 Jan/Feb issue of *Ministries* magazine. The report is given by Loren Cunningham, founder of Youth With A Mission.

> According to the U.S. Center For World Mission, more than 22,000 Chinese are coming to Christ each day. That is the equivalent of seven days of Pentecost every 24 hours and it is happening right now. Most of this explosion of new belief is coming from China's rural communities, where 80% of the population of China lives. When I was in Hong Kong not long ago, Jonathan Chao, founder of the Chinese Church Research Center, told me how the Chinese Revival is being spread by young people, mostly ages 15 to 19. The teenagers go to villages and share the gospel where it has never been heard before. As converts are organized into small groups, the teens call for the "elders" (believers in their twenties) to come and teach the newly formed home church while the younger Christians go on to reach the next village. Chinese pastors and teachers don't have financial impediments to spreading the Christian message: they live with the peasant farmers in each new area and don't construct buildings. They have very little and need very little. By this simple means the good news is leaping across the fields and mountains of China.

The explosive Church growth that is now going on in China and that which attended the early Church in the book of Acts had something in common: they were both a house church movement. This same kind of growth is seen in other countries today where church buildings are not allowed, as we saw in John Amstutz's letter.

The principle, simply expressed, is that the growth of the Church in any given area will be in direct proportion to the number of obstacles that we allow to hinder the planting of new churches. From my experience in both planting and pastoring house churches, I see some definite advantages to this approach to church planting and church multiplication.

Consider the following:

House Churches are Easy to Start

To plant a house church:
- You do not need to buy property
- Or build a building
- You won't need a pulpit
- Or pews
- Or hymn books
- Or a piano
- You can do without a baptistry
- A Sunday School
- A youth pastor
- You won't have to belong to a denomination
- Or be incorporated
- Or meet on Sundays
- Or have a church bulletin
- Or meet in the same place every week

You won't need a sign with the name of your church on it. It won't need a name. In fact, you don't even have to call it a *church* as long as you know that it is "the Church, which is His Body." None of the above are bad or wrong, but neither are they essential. The Apostle Paul used none of them in his church-planting ministry. **We have left the simplicity of the New Testament and have added too many extras.** The more non-essentials we add, the more difficult we make it to start a new church.

Ray Williams, a close personal friend, has been a missionary in Mexico for over thirty years and has been instrumental in starting scores of churches out of which hundreds more have been planted. He told me recently that he once started a church in a wheat field. That church has grown, and out of it have come other churches, each with a church planting vision. We make it too complicated. God is calling us back to simplicity.

A House Church is Relaxed and Informal

Several years ago, I took my family to a church whose pastor was an outstanding Bible teacher. We loved the church and wanted to continue to attend but the dress code was completely out of our reach. Some people do not come to our churches today because we have set the standard of dress too high and made church a *formal* event. Many people who will not attend a formal church will attend a house church, because it is more relaxed with a casual family setting.

In his book *Understanding Church Growth*, Dr. Donald McGavran lists "Eight Keys to Church Growth in Cities." The very first one gives us his assessment of the value and importance of planting and multiplying house churches.

> The eight keys I am about to mention are not mere guesses. They describe principles about which church growth men are agreed. First, emphasize house churches. When the Church begins to grow in cities among non-Christians, each congregation must soon find a place to assemble. The congregation should meet in the most natural surroundings, to which non-Christians can come with the greatest ease and where the converts themselves carry on the services. Obtaining a place to assemble should not lay a financial burden on the little congregation. The house church meets all these requirements ideally. House churches should always be considered, both for initial planting and for later extension.

House Churches are Evangelistic Tools

Dr. Peter Wagner, considered by many to be the foremost authority on Church growth today, says, "The best method under heaven for evangelism is church planting. There never was a better method and there never will be." Saturation church planting is the vision now being adopted by mission leaders worldwide.

Churches that divide in order to multiply will experience addition. Our goal has too often been to try to make one very large congregation rather than to multiply congregations. We cannot say that God would never lead anyone to build a very large congregation. However, the Body of Christ in any city will increase much more rapidly by multiplying congregations than it will by seeking to build a few super churches. We praise God for the super churches. We pray for them, and we bless them. It is not *us and them*. It is US! The whole Body of Christ belongs to all of us, and we belong to each other. There is not one way to extend the Kingdom of God — there are many ways, and it is our responsibility to know what methods God is leading us to use.

House Churches Facilitate
the Training of Pastors and Elders

Educators have long understood that the best method of training is still the apprentice method. This one-on-one, hands-on training is such as a blacksmith, plumber, or lawyer would have received two hundred years ago. They learned by observing and doing, while being accountable to a master in the trade. This was Jesus' method. His disciples learned by watching, listening, and doing while they lived their lives with the Master Teacher himself. House churches will enable us to train pastors to actually do the work of pastoring while they are under the supervision of a more experienced pastor. They will grow as the church grows under their leadership. Some will pastor more than one house church since they will not all meet on Sunday morning.

House Churches Help Bond Relationships

A small house church makes it much more likely that the very shy will find their identity within the Body of Christ. In our house church we usually have our noon meal together on Sundays. Each family takes part by bringing a covered dish or some part of the meal. The forming of relationships occurs much more easily in such household situations.

House Churches are Economical

A house church will be able to channel almost all of its finances into missions and mercy ministries. Some of our house churches channel ninety-three percent of their offerings into local benevolence and foreign missions. There may be some minor expenses; but since the meetings are held in houses, all building expenses are avoided.

Meetings can be held on other days or nights, as well as Sundays. Nothing in the New Testament says that Sunday is the time for church. As a matter of fact, the pattern in the book of Acts is that they met daily. The first day of the week is seldom mentioned at all, and never is it emphasized as a special day set aside for worship. The apostle Paul discouraged a "special day" mentality in Galatians 4:10-11:

> You are observing special days and months and seasons and years. I fear for you, that somehow I have wasted my efforts on you.

Many of these house churches will be led by pastors having regular full-time jobs. While the honor of a livable income should go to those who are giving full-time to the work, it is also true that those pastors who serve part-time should receive similar honor to offset expenses and to encourage them in the work of the ministry. The workman is worthy of his hire, whether part-time or full-time. Men (and women) should not wait until they can be freed from a full-time job before they begin to serve as pastors. The apostle Paul worked with his hands often — not only to meet his own needs, but also the needs of those who traveled with him.

> You yourselves know that these hands of mine have supplied my own needs and the needs of my companions. In everything I did, I showed you that by this kind of hard work we must help the weak, remembering the words the Lord Jesus himself said: "It is more blessed to give than receive" (Acts 20:34-35).

House Churches can Solve the Problem of Growth

Some churches grow so large that they have to build bigger buildings or rent more space or have two services. This is what we call a *happy problem*. There is also a happy solution: begin to train pastors by assigning them an area of the city and sending off two or three families to start a house church in that section of the city. The most life-giving thing a church can do is to have a baby. Churches die because of a spirit of possessiveness in the leadership. God will bless the people who are continually giving away everything that God gives them. Jesus said, "*Give and it shall be given to you.*" A giving church is a growing church.

Michael Green, principal of St. John's College of Nottingham, England, addressed the International Congress on World Evangelization in Lausanne, Switzerland, in 1974. Speaking on "Methods and Strategy in the Evangelism of the Early Church," he said:

> In the early Church, buildings were unimportant. They did not have any during the period of their greatest advance. Today they seem all-important to many Christians; their upkeep consumes the money and interest of the members, often plunges them into debt, and isolates them from those who do not go to church. Indeed, even the word has changed meaning. *Church* no longer means a company of people, as it did in New Testament times. These days it means a building.

The fastest growing movements in history have always been those that have not bogged down under ponderous organizational structures and have focused on essentials without wavering.

THREE

The House Church
in the
New Testament

The Scripture passages below show that common, ordinary dwellings were used for discipling new converts both during Jesus' lifetime as well as during the expansion of the New Testament Church in the book of Acts.

A House Where Jesus is Worshiped

> On coming to the house, they saw the child with his mother, Mary, and they bowed down and worshiped him. Then they opened their treasures and presented him with gifts of gold and of incense and myrrh (Matthew 2:11).

The very first time a group gathered to worship Jesus and offer him gifts was in a house, the house of Mary and Joseph.

A House Used for a Healing Meeting

> When Jesus came into Peter's house, He saw Peter's
> mother-in-law lying in a bed with a fever. He touched her
> hand and the fever left her, and she got up and began to
> wait on Him. When evening came, many who were
> demon possessed were brought to Him and He drove out
> the spirits and healed all their sick (Matthew 8:14-16).

In the early days of his ministry, Jesus used the house of
Peter to conduct preaching, healing, and deliverance
meetings.

A House Where the First
Communion Service is Held

In the last week of Jesus' ministry he said to His disciples,

> Go into the city to a certain man and tell him, "The
> teacher says: My appointed time is near. I am going to
> celebrate the Passover with My disciples at your house"
> (Matthew 26:18).

Our Lord could have chosen to celebrate the first
communion with His disciples in a synagogue, in the temple,
or in some other place of religious significance — but He
chose to celebrate it in an ordinary house. Thus, He set His
seal on the common dwelling place as a holy and sanctified
place, worthy of the most solemn worship services.

A House Where Jesus Preached to Crowds

> Several days later he returned to Capernaum, and the
> news of His arrival spread quickly through the city. Soon
> the house where He was staying was so packed with
> visitors that there wasn't room for a single person more,
> not even outside the door. And He preached the word to
> them (Mark 2:1 Living Bible).

The things we do in our church buildings today are the things Jesus did in houses, in the open air, and in the temple courtyard during his public ministry.

Pentecost Came to a House Church

> When the day of Pentecost came, they were all together in one place. Suddenly a sound like the blowing of a violent wind came from heaven and filled the whole house where they were sitting (Acts 2:1-2).

Have we ever considered the number of foundational events that took place in someone's house.

- The first worship service was in a house.

- The first communion service was in a house.

- Jesus preached and healed the sick in a house.

- The gospel was first preached to the Gentiles in the house of Cornelius.

- The outpouring of the Holy Spirit on the day of Pentecost happened in a house.

- And the first churches that the Apostle Paul started were all in houses.

Over the centuries we have lost the dynamic of simplicity and have added things that have slowed the progress of the Church into all nations.

In the Streets and in the Houses

> They worshiped together regularly at the Temple each day, met in small groups in homes for communion and shared their meals with great joy and thankfulness (Acts 2:46).

The early Church not only met as small groups in homes but also as larger crowds in public places. The most rapid growth of the Church — both in the past and in the present — has been when the Church was not using formal meeting places, remaining flexible, mobile, and aggressive.

Saul Attacks the House Churches

> But Saul began ravaging the church, entering house after house: and dragging off men and women, he would put them in prison (Acts 8:3).

Where did Saul of Tarsus go to find "the people of the way" to drag them to prison and to death? He found them meeting in houses. He himself would later plant churches in houses on his missionary journeys.

A Praying House Church
Delivers Peter from Prison

> Day after day in the temple courts and from house to house they never stopped teaching and proclaiming the news that Jesus is the Christ (Acts 5:42).

They did not meet in the temple proper, but rather on the temple grounds, or in the vicinity of the temple where the people were gathered. This was an open-air meeting. *The History of Christianity* by Lion states that,

> Christians had no special buildings but met in private houses. Justin Martyr A.D. 100–165 was asked by Rusticus the Prefect: "Where do you assemble?" Justin said, "Where each one chooses and can, or do you fancy that we all meet in the very same place? Not so, because the God of the Christians is not circumscribed by space."

In his book *Cells For Life*, Ron Trudinger says,

> They initiated the practice of meeting daily in the temple and of breaking of bread from house to house. This term can also be rendered: "In the various private homes." Synagogues were used for a while, but as we see in Acts 19, it was not long before many of these were closed to Christians. But we continue to find significant references in Acts and the Epistles to churches in homes.

A House Church Opened the Gospel to the Nations

> The following day Peter arrived in Caesarea. Cornelius was expecting them and called together his relatives and close friends. As Peter entered the house, Cornelius met him and fell at his feet in reverence. Peter went inside and found a large gathering of people (Acts 10:24-27).

This is a good example of how to start a house church. Someone who is hungry for God and for the things of God calls together a number of his family and friends to come and hear the Word of God. So simple! This meeting in the house of Cornelius was historic. It was the breakthrough that convinced the Jewish believers that the Good News was for all the nations of the world and not just for the Jews.

Lydia's House was Europe's First Church

> After Paul and Silas came out of the prison, they went to Lydia's house where they met with the brothers and encouraged them (Acts 16:40).

The Church of Philippi was formed in the house of Lydia. We are not told how the church grew. But when the group could no longer fit in Lydia's house, they probably formed another group somewhere in the city and continued to divide and multiply.

Paul's Rented House was a House Church

> For two whole years Paul stayed in his own rented house and welcomed all who came to see him. Boldly and without hindrance he preached the kingdom of God and taught about the Lord Jesus Christ (Acts 28:30-31).

These final words in the book of Acts reveal that Paul not only made use of the homes of others for the proclamation of the gospel, but that he also used his own rented house for spreading the good news of God's love. The fastest growing movement in the world today, the Christian movement, began in houses. **It had its greatest growth while it remained a fluid, simple, mobile, relationship-oriented people.**

From Shadow to Substance

All the types and shadows of the Old Testament were totally fulfilled in Christ. We no longer need the tabernacle, the vestments, the temple, the furniture, or any such thing. "Christ is all and in all. We are Complete in Him." We no longer need a holy place, or an altar of incense or a laver, or shewbread, or umim, or thummim. We don't need the shadows for we have the substance. **His name is Jesus!**

A Samaritan woman said to Jesus,

> "Sir, our fathers worshiped on this mountain, but you Jews claim that the place where we must worship is in Jerusalem." Jesus declared, "Believe me, woman, a time is coming when you will worship the Father, neither on this mountain, nor in Jerusalem. You Samaritans worship what you do not know; we worship what we do know, for salvation is from the Jews. Yet a time is coming and now is come when the true worshippers will worship the Father in spirit and truth, for they are the kind of worshippers the Father seeks. God is spirit and his worshippers must worship in spirit and in truth" (John 4:20-24).

Jesus made it clear that the time had come, and that Jerusalem was no more a *holy place* than Samaria. For **He had come,** and in His coming he forever brought an end to the idea of holy places. He Himself had fulfilled all the types and shadows of the Old Testament.

Let us rejoice and praise the Lord that we have been released from all bondage and legalism regarding the place where we are supposed to worship God! We are free to worship Him alone or together, anytime day or night, in any place we choose.

FOUR

What is
a Church?

The original Greek word *ekklesia* is composed of two words: *ek*, meaning "out of" or "out from," and *kalleo*, meaning "I call." The meaning of *church* according to the original word is "I call out from." When Jesus said, "I will build my Church," He was saying, "I will call My people out of the world and they will assemble in My name, and the gates of Hell shall not prevail against them." This implies that Jesus' called-out people will rally as an army of love and grace to take the world for Him, and the enemy will not be able to stop the advance. This invincible army will be motivated by the love of God within their hearts and by the message of love and forgiveness on their lips.

Actually *ekklessia* has two meanings: that of being called out, and that of being assembled together. We cannot experience church until we come together. My wife and I are one, even when we are separated from each other by many miles. But we do not experience the full benefits and blessings of our marriage union until we are together. Even so, you and every other believer in your city constitute the church in that city, even when you are not assembled. But we cannot receive the benefits and blessings of church until we come together. This, of course, does not mean that we all have to be in the same place at the same time. That will probably never happen in any city.

Not a Religious Word

I was amazed and delighted recently to discover that the word *ekklesia* in the New Testament was not a religious word at all. I was reading through the nineteenth chapter of Acts where the apostle Paul was threatened by an angry mob that wanted to kill him. The writer uses several different words to describe this mob: *the whole city, the people, the crowd,* and three times he uses the word *assembly.*

> The **assembly** was in confusion: Some were shouting one thing, some another. Most of the people did not even know why they were there . . . The city clerk quieted the crowd and said, "Men of Ephesus . . . if Demetrius and his fellow craftsmen have a grievance against anybody, the courts are open and there are proconsuls . . . If there is anything further you want to bring up, it must be settled in a legal **assembly** . . . " After he had said this he dismissed the **assembly** (Acts 19:28-41).

The remarkable thing about the above passage is that the word *assembly* in the original language is *ekklesia,* which is the word we always translate *church.* So Jesus used a common word when He said, "I will build my Church." It was not a religious word. It simply meant a called-out group, or crowd, or fellowship, or assembly. So we can use the word *church* when it communicates what we are saying, but we can also use the word *fellowship, gathering, brethren, saints, disciples, college,* or *believers.* It simply means a group of people — a group of God's people.

John Dawson, in his book *Taking Our Cities for God,* said:

> There is no absolute model for what a local church should be. I once spent an afternoon with over one hundred spiritual leaders from several denominations. We tried to come up with a universal definition of a Biblical local church. You may think that it was an easy task, but if you consider all the cultures and circumstances

of people on the earth and you examine the diversity of models in the Bible, you will begin to understand our frustration. After many hours of discussion, we had produced many good models, but no absolute definition other than "people moving together under the Lordship of Jesus."

I like that definition, but I really believe the Lord has given us a very good definition of the local church as well as the universal Church. It is found in Ephesians 1:22-23.

And God placed all things under His feet and appointed Him to be head over everything for the Church, which is His body, the fullness of Him who fills everything in every way.

Throughout the New Testament, both the local church and the universal Church is called *the Church*. The local body, no matter how small or how large, is called *the church*, and the whole worldwide Body of Christ is also called *the Church*. The Church is Jesus' body whether it is gathered or scattered. This simply means that wherever there is a group of Christians gathered there is *the Church*.

I was born and raised in Texas. At Christmas, we would go out into the country and cut our own Christmas tree. It was a Christmas tree the minute we cut it and took it to the house. We would then put it on a stand and decorate it with a whole lot of little ornaments to make the tree look bright and festive. But, even if we had shaken all the ornaments off, it would still have been your basic Christmas tree.

If God were to shake everything loose until there was nothing left but a simple, basic New Testament Church, what would He have left? In other words, if I take away all the extras and the non-essentials and cut away all the frills from what I understand to be church, what would remain? It is our purpose in this chapter to answer that question. But first let us examine the word *parachurch*.

What is Parachurch?

Recently I read a book that sought to explain the nature of the Church. Under the title "What is the Relationship of the Church to Other Parachurch Organizations?" the author made the following observation:

> The Bible is clear that it is through the vehicle, or instrument, of the Church that God is going to accomplish His great purpose. However, because the church has not always been what it was supposed to be, many have become discouraged with the church's ability to meet certain obvious needs. For this reason, caring and concerned individuals have, over the years, established missionary societies, orphanages, Christian businessmen's organizations and other like institutions to meet these pressing needs. As God continues to restore and strengthen His Church, the need for these organizations will diminish and the church will be ministering to these needs.

It is obvious in the above quote that the writer felt strongly that parachurch is not church, and that something less than church had come along to meet certain needs until the real Church could be healed or awakened to do the work it ought to be doing. This is an example of the error of thinking that if it does not look like church it is not church. The fact is that when a parachurch organization is made up of born-again believers in Jesus who are come together to serve and worship Him, it is not parachurch, *it is church!* **Church is people.** It is not organization, institution, or denomination. It would be difficult to find a true parachurch organization. For if it were composed of Christians, it would not be parachurch, it would be CHURCH — God's called-out people! Even if some members were not born-again, it would still be church, for what church is there without some unsaved people in attendance?

A few years ago I had the same idea about parachurch. In my teaching ministry I would often say, "If the church were doing what it ought to be doing, we wouldn't need all these parachurch organizations." It never occurred to me that these parachurch people were people of God and were just as much the Church, the Body of Christ — moving together under the Lordship of Jesus — as we were, even though the building they met in was not shaped like ours.

Our oldest son has been a member of a well-known *parachurch* organization for many years. They are doing an outstanding job in missions and evangelism and are growing rapidly all over the world. A few years ago, while we were discussing his future and his association with this particular organization, I shared that I had some serious misgivings about the organization because it was not a church but a parachurch organization. He seemed apologetic and agreed with me fully that what he and others were doing in that organization, though it was being wonderfully blessed of God, was still not God's perfect will because it was not happening through a church but rather through a parachurch. He also was confused about church and so-called parachurch.

A day or two later I was driving along thinking about our conversation when I felt the Lord gently asking me: "What is it that makes an organization a church?" As I tried to answer that question, I felt God gave me a revelation. I had never before seen so clearly as I did in that moment of time that an organization is not a church because it has been recognized by a denominational headquarters as a church; it is not a church because it has regular Sunday morning services and practices baptism and the Lord's Supper. It is not a church because it meets on a regular basis or in a particular location. It is church simply because it is God's called-out people moving together under the Lordship of Jesus.

Alfred Kuen, in his book *I Will Build My Church*, published by Moody Press in 1971, says on page fifty-one, under the heading "When is a Local Church a Church?"

> It is easy to get bogged down with peripheral issues and questions. And there does not seem to be a clear-cut way to define a local church. For example, is it when you have a constitution and hold regular meetings? Is it when you have baptized believers who partake regularly of the Lord's Supper? Is it when you have church officers, such as elders and deacons? Should numerous norms be present in order to have a local church? It certainly does

not include a certain level of maturity: for the Corinthians were yet carnal, but Paul called them a church. Further, it does not seem necessary to have spiritual leaders before you call a body of believers a church, for it is clearly implied in Acts 14:21-22 that groups of believers throughout Lystra, Iconium and Antioch were called churches even before elders were appointed.

When, then, can a body of believers be called a church? I personally tend toward a simple definition: a body of believers can be called a church whenever that group meets together regularly for mutual edification. Jesus said, in the context of talking about church discipline, "For where two or three are gathered together in my name, there am I in the midst of them" (Matthew 18:20 KJV). And it is clear what Tertullian, one of the early church fathers felt Jesus meant, for he said: "Where there are two or three believers, even laymen, there is a church."

Jim Montgomery, in his book *Dawn — 2000; Seven Million Churches to Go*, says,

I'm impressed with how a group of Christians faced this most fundamental question in China. They said, concerning this question, many older Christians said that they could not predict the future form of Chinese churches. So they turned to the Bible for an answer. They found in the Bible that the house-church form was a legitimate church . . . we found a book by Wan Ming-dao (perhaps the most highly respected believer in China, who languished in jail for more than twenty years) on the institution of the church. He held that where there were Christians, there was a church. We were happy about this. We assumed that although our group consisted of only a few people, we actually were a church whose head was Jesus. "Where there are Christians, there is a church," is a profound definition coming from a Church growing rapidly and laboring under the most difficult of circumstance.

A Congregation of Believers is a Church

Some time ago I was teaching a small group of believers in the village of La Rumurosa in Old Mexico. I was explaining Matthew 18:20, *"Where two or three are gathered together in my name, I am in the midst of them."* A word in the Spanish translation of that verse leaped out at me. I had not seen it before. It says, "Donde hay dos o tres CONGREGADOS en mi nombre, alli estoy en medio de ellos." Where two or three are congregated in My name, there am I in the midst of them. I asked the group, "According to this verse, how many does it take to make a congregation?" As I waited for them to answer, I was struck with the weight of the answer that was forming in my own mind. Two or three is all it takes to make a congregation and a congregation of believers with Jesus in its midst is church! Not just two or three people, but two or three who are called by His Name because they belong to Him.

Jesus in the Midst

Jesus within is the experience of the individual in his own private walk with the Lord. *Jesus in the midst* is the church mode. It is Jesus walking among us, touching us, speaking to us through the gifts of the Spirit flowing through the members of His Body, the Church. *Jesus in the midst* is the corporate experience. *Jesus within* is the private experience. When two or three born-again believers come together in His name, Jesus is *in the midst.* Jesus in the midst is CHURCH! It is a different experience than Jesus within. We cannot experience Jesus in the midst while we are alone. We can only experience Jesus in the midst when we are in company with others; at least one or two others who are called by His name.

But is it a church in the fullest sense of the word? Yes, it is church in the fullest sense of the word. It is the basic church. You can have more than two or three and it is still church — church in the fullest sense. But it does not become more of a church because there are more than two or three people in the congregation. It only becomes a bigger church.

The Role of Church Leaders

But what about pastors, deacons, teachers, apostles, evangelists, and bishops? Is it church without these being present? Yes, it is church, even without all of the above. The fourth chapter of Ephesians says that the Lord gave to the Church all these ministries, but He gave these gifts to the Church. If God gives these gifts to the Church, it is evident that the Church can exist and does exist before these gifts are given to it.

When Paul went out on his first missionary journey, he established churches in four cities. On his way back to Antioch he ordained elders for those churches. This indicates that they were churches before leadership was appointed. Consider the following:

> They returned again to Lystra, and to Iconium and Antioch, confirming the souls of the disciples, and exhorting them to continue in the faith, and that we must through much tribulation enter into the kingdom of God. And when they had ordained them elders in every church, and had prayed with fasting, they commended them to the Lord, on whom they had believed" (Acts 14:21-23).

The elders were added to the churches (disciples). Disciples called by God out of darkness into light are the Church! The writer of Acts uses the words *disciples* and *church* interchangeably.

Paul felt it safe to leave these newly-formed churches in the hands of the Lord on whom the people had believed. This is a key statement. We, who are placed into leadership, have taken too much upon ourselves in assuming that the church cannot function without our constant watch-care over the flock. The word *bishop* simply means overseer. A bishop is an overseer and a feeder and functions as a father or a nurse to his children. But there is a limit to our spiritual oversight, which we have too often violated. The major violation by church leaders in our day is that we have almost completely taken the initiative away from the people and have invested it into a professional clergy.

Then What is a Church?

If we take away all the non-essentials, we would have Jesus and at least two people who have come together in His name. Two people, who have been born-again, meeting together anywhere, at anytime, with Jesus in the midst, is church at its most basic, most informal level. This, of course, does not mean that this essential level is where the Lord wants us to operate all the time. Praise God for larger groups. But let us never lose sight of the basic church. If we do, we will tend to lapse into forms, rituals, ceremonies, religiosity, institutionalism, legalism, and stagnation.

FIVE

What is a House Church?

The characteristics listed below are those of the Church for the first 250 years of Church history. When the Church moved away from simplicity, it also moved away from much of its power and flexibility in evangelizing and discipling the nations. These are also the characteristics of most house churches springing up all over the world today.

A House Church is a Simple Church

No frills. No ceremony. No rituals. No symbolism. It is simply a time for the people of God to come together with Jesus in the midst. They talk. They sing. They pray. They eat a meal together. They baptize new converts, take communion together, and study the Bible. They share what God is doing in their lives. They intercede for people and for all kinds of needs all over the world. They minister to one another through the gifts God has given each one. They love one another and seek to encourage and build each other up in their faith.

A House Church Meets in a House

The home is an easy place to have church. There are no mysterious emblems to explain. It is not a religious setting. No one feels uncomfortable about doing something irreligious. People feel at home and just relax. Church starts the minute the first two or three people arrive because church is people and not program. Where born-again believers gather, there is a church. They are the *church gathered*. When they all leave, they are the *church scattered*. They come together to be strengthened. They go out to touch the world as salt, light, and leaven in the power of the Holy Spirit. They go everywhere preaching the gospel through words and deeds to those who do not know Jesus. They are fulfilling the Great Commission which says, *As you are going, here, there, and everywhere, preach the gospel at all times, wherever you happen to be . . . now* (cf. Matthew 10:7, Mark 16:15, 20).

A House Church is a Center of Evangelism

It is easier to get an unsaved person to visit a meeting in someone's house than it is to get him to go into a "sanctuary." This is one of the reasons the Church of the First Century turned the world upside-down.

A House Church Makes Discipleship Easier

It is good to knock on doors and lead people to Jesus. It is good to lead them to the Lord on the streets, in the parks, in huge stadiums, over the phone, or in casual conversation. But when we lead him to the Lord right in the place where he will be discipled — a church in a house — we have a distinct advantage. He has already been introduced to the church. He can be baptized right on the spot and led gently into a deeper walk with Jesus by the people who led him to receive Christ. The task of getting him into a church is already done.

A House Church Relates to the Entire Body of Christ

The only name that is worthy of lifting up is the name of Jesus. We don't need to think up a good name for our church. It is not our church. It is Jesus' church. It is "the church that meets at someone's house." It is a part of the city-wide church. Everything that belongs to Jesus belongs to His church. Everything that Jesus is doing in our city is ours. We all have some responsibility toward it even if it is to pray and nothing more. We are one body. We are born into unity, and we maintain that unity by receiving all the saints without regard to where they live or what group they attend. We all belong to each other.

A House Church is Movable

We do not have to meet at the same house every week. It is not the building that holds us together. It is relationships that bond us together. We are flexible. We can meet anywhere. In this way we are exposing ourselves to more people in more places.

A House Church is Small

Big is not always better. Big, however, is what we want. But we can get bigger faster by multiplying than we can by adding. A house church builds the big, city-wide church by dividing and multiplying. We will have large gatherings from time to time, but our basic church is still small. When more than twenty or thirty people attend consistently, it is time to *have a baby.*

A House Church is *the Church*

We read of the Church on four different levels in the New Testament. The Church in the world (Colossians 1:24), the church in the province (Acts 9:31), the church in the city (2 Corinthians 1:1), and the church in the house (Colossians 4:15). The church in the house is a microcosm of the church in the city, in the nation, and in the world. The church in the house is just as much *the church* as the church in the city, or in the province, or in the world. It contains all of the essential elements of church. The word *microcosm* simply means "little world" or "a universe in miniature." The church in the house is *church* in the fullest sense of the word. That is how the Apostle Paul saw his work in the First Century. On his first missionary journey, he left a little group of disciples in four different cities —Antioch, Iconium, Derby, and Lystra. He referred to each little group as the church in that city.

A House Church in New Testament Practice

I did not say *New Testament Pattern*, for God did not leave us a pattern to be followed as to how to conduct church. The true New Testament pattern is to pray, hear from God, and obey what He tells us. If He tells you to build a gigantic cathedral, you must obey and do what He says. You will be blessed and so will the entire Body of Christ. The dynamic power of the early church was just that. They were not trying to follow a "pattern" that they read about somewhere. They were following the leading of the Holy Spirit day by day. Success followed. It is still safe to do the same in our day. Many churches have tried to find the formula for growth that Pastor Cho of Seoul, Korea, found and used to build the largest church in the world. Pastor Cho shared that formula in six simple words: "I just pray, and I obey." There is nothing wrong with meeting in a barn, a field, a cave, in a church building, or in a synagogue. The Lord is looking on the heart. But if we are encouraging a system that is stifling the life of the church by heavy-handed leadership and a deadening clergy-laity caste system, we will not have the fruit we are seeking.

House Churches are Easy to Start

Church planting is a means of evangelism, discipleship, and missions. It has been proven in the church growth movement that the best method of evangelism is planting lots of churches. The best way to make disciples is also to start lots of new churches. When people gather in small, informal groups, discipleship takes place almost without a conscious effort. And it's not hard to start a new church! You only need two or three people and someone to host a small gathering each week in their home.

House Churches can Start
Before the Church Planter Arrives

The churches in Antioch and Samaria started up before the apostles arrived. Also in the tenth chapter of Acts, Cornelius was instrumental in starting a house church without even knowing what he was doing. This is happening in China and in many other places in our day. This does not rule out the work of apostles, prophets, evangelists and pastor/teachers. We are talking about starting churches, not the ongoing success of these churches. We will need the ministry of anointed leaders appointed by the Lord if these churches are to succeed.

These are some of the characteristics of house churches. Every house church will have its own personality. No two meetings will be alike. It is the Spirit of Jesus Who guides us in all our gatherings. He brings all the excitement of His presence into each meeting by using anyone He chooses to minister.

SIX

Church
Membership

Have you made the delightful discovery that you are a member of every church in town? If you belong to Jesus you are a member of His Body, whatever church you attend — whether your name is on the roll or not. This thought may be startling at first, but after comparing it with certain statements in the book of Acts we see that it is true.

- Acts 2:41 — "Those who accepted his message were baptized and about 3,000 were **added to their number."**

- Acts 2:47 — ". . . and the Lord **added to their number** those who were being saved."

- Acts 4:4 — "And **the number grew** to about 5,000."

- Acts 5:12-14 — "And all the believers in Jerusalem used to meet together in Solomon's Colonnade. No one else dared join them . . . nevertheless, more and more men and women believed in the Lord and **were added to their number."**

- Acts 5:42-6:1 — "Day after day, in the temple courts and from house to house, they never stopped teaching and proclaiming the good news that Jesus is the Christ. In those days . . . **the number of disciples was increasing.**"

- Acts 8:1-3 — "On that day a great persecution broke out against **the Church at Jerusalem** . . . Saul began to destroy **the church.** Going from house to house he dragged off men and women and put them in prison."

As we meditate on the passages above, some facts become evident:

1. The thousands of believers scattered throughout the city of Jerusalem were called *the Church.* They had a very clear understanding that, even though they met in a multitude of tiny congregations in houses all over the city which were also called *churches,* there was in fact, only one Body of Christ in the City of Jerusalem called *the Church.*

2. The Lord was the one who added people to the Church. There is no indication that there was a membership roll or list of members for each individual congregation. Throughout the New Testament there is never the slightest hint of a local congregation making up a membership roll of those who were exclusively members of that particular group. On the contrary, the idea is always clearly presented that all the believers in the entire city were members one of another, because they were members of the Body of Christ in that place.

3. The only qualification for being added to the number was being born-again. *"The Lord added to their number those who were being saved"* (Acts 2:47). To add anything else as a condition for becoming a member of a local fellowship is totally without Scriptural grounds and is a direct challenge to the Holy Spirit who has already added every born-again believer to the number of disciples in that city. We are members of Jesus' body the moment we are born-again. Moreover, we have no grounds whatsoever to call some who attend our

meetings *members* and some *non-members*. Every person who is saved is a member of Jesus' body and therefore a member of the congregation of believers he is presently attending. As a matter of fact, he is a member of every local congregation in the city, because all the local congregations together make up the Body of Christ in that place.

4. Although the Church in Jerusalem had many local congregations meeting in homes, they all came together in the temple courts for larger public gatherings. We read of the Church scattered into small gatherings in houses for nurturing as well as larger gatherings in public places.

5. In all the references above, *the number* refers to all the believers throughout Jerusalem. The phrase *the number* and *the church* are used interchangeably. This makes it clear that when the Lord adds you to *the number* He is adding you to *the Church* of which there is only one for the entire city. This does not contradict the fact that there were many house churches throughout the city which made up the city-wide church. The practice of making up a *membership roll* has no precedent in the New Testament. It is a device that has become a snare and has been used by the enemy to further divide the Body of Christ into isolated compartments throughout the city. It encourages division among God's people rather than unity.

We have been taught that you owe your loyalty, your allegiance, your time, your talents, and your tithe to one church and to no other. In other words, once you are a member of a particular church you cannot be a member of any other church — as if attending or helping another congregation of God's people would in some way be disloyalty to Christ.

We must separate the two issues of membership and commitment. They are not the same issue. I can be a member of every church in town and still honor all my commitments to teach, lead, labor, give, and assist in various congregations throughout the city. I can fulfill all my commitments to any part of the Body of Christ without having to restrict myself to attending only one fellowship of believers.

Everything that belongs to Christ within the city belongs to every believer within the city. Any other view leads to a spirit of competition, jealousy, and sectarianism, which is heresy. For this reason it is wrong to call anyone a *church tramp* or a *church hopper* or a *grasshopper* or a *butterfly* or any other derogatory name just because he or she may attend and function in more than one congregation.

This brings us to another word that has been used to strike fear into anyone who would dare try to "steal sheep." The awesome, chilling word is *proselytizing*. The word *proselyte* is found four times in the Bible. It means "an arriver from a foreign region," i.e., a convert to Judaism. This word can never be used to describe Christians who attend and serve more than one fellowship.

In the first place, none of these sheep belong to any pastor. They belong to Jesus. Every apostle, prophet, evangelist, and pastor is only to watch over, protect, and feed Jesus' sheep. They are not to possess them as their own. One may say, "But as a pastor, I am commissioned to protect them from danger." That is true when it comes to protecting them from heresy or from Satan's snares, but it certainly does not mean that they are to be protected from each other! We need to encourage fellowship among the saints within the city who make up the Body of Christ. And who gave us the idea that it was only the pastors who had any responsibility over the sheep? God gave all five gifts to bring the sheep into maturity, not just the gift of pastor. The apostle, the prophet, the teacher, and the evangelist have the same responsibility as the pastor in bringing God's people up to maturity.

In the second place, the word *proselyte* can only mean bringing a person out of one religion into another, not from one Christian congregation into another. The word is never used in the Bible in that sense. You cannot proselytize a Christian unless you take him out of Christianity into another religion. This word cannot apply to the free migration of the sheep from one Christian shepherd to another. It is the privilege of the sheep to seek spiritual nurture and guidance from any of God's shepherds at any time or place. And it is the duty of every pastor (shepherd) to nurture and guide any and all of God's sheep that come to him for help. Let us never be guilty of trying to rope Jesus' sheep into our fold and brand them with our particular brand. They belong to Jesus and can find pasture through any of his under-shepherds, anywhere, anytime. For those who may resent being called sheep, just remember that we are all called sheep, including the shepherds. "We are the sheep of His pasture" (Psalm 100).

How Not to Produce Loyalty

"But if I don't have a membership roll with some basic requirements, such as tithing, faithful attendance, godly living, witnessing, etc., how will I ever have faithful people?"

Such a question exposes the error of a system that produces pure legalism. Do we think that we can produce spiritual maturity in our people by binding them to some kind of legal code of ethics, using membership as leverage? This gets close to the Roman Catholic Church's practice of selling Indulgences a few hundred years ago. Are we selling church membership by making up a set of requirements that include regular giving of the tithe?

Let us just receive everyone who attends our meetings and work with him to develop spiritual maturity to whatever extent he is willing to follow our leadership. That will take all the pressure off of both you and him and do away with first-class and second-class citizens. They will all be on the same level. And if, while they are attending your gatherings, they are also attending other meetings, praise the Lord that they are hungry enough to want more than you can give them and pray for the other pastor or leader who is helping you feed Jesus' sheep.

The charge of proselytizing should never be heard among true, God-called pastors. Any shepherd who seeks to lure sheep unto himself for selfish or greedy purposes will answer to the Lord for his sin. Throughout the New Testament the shepherds were directed to relate to the whole flock and the people were directed to relate to the elders of the city-wide church, not just one elder. Consider Hebrews 13:7 and 17:

> Remember your leaders [plural] . . . and submit to their authority. They keep watch over you as men [plural] who must give an account . . .

And Acts 20:17 and 28:

> Paul sent to Ephesus for the elders of the church. When they arrived, he said to them, "Keep watch over yourselves and all the flock of which the Holy Spirit has made you overseers. Be shepherds of the Church of God, which He bought with His own blood."

In Hebrews 13, the saints were admonished to relate to all spiritual authority, not just to a certain elder. And in Acts 20, Paul reminds all the elders that they, collectively, are to watch over the flock (singular) in the city of Ephesus. In those days they understood that all the elders within a city had some measure of responsibility to all the saints within that city.

In all of the New Testament there is not one example of a single pastor overseeing a single congregation. The Holy Spirit gave pastors, teachers, evangelists, prophets, and apostles to oversee the whole Church, not just one little compartment of the Church. If the apostle, prophet, evangelist, and teacher can function in this mode — and they do — why can't the pastor? It is no more difficult for the pastor to relate to more than one congregation than it is for the prophet, apostle, evangelist, and teacher. It is the healthiest way for the church to function.

In Acts 20:29-30, Paul went on to say to the shepherds in Ephesus,

> I know that after I leave, savage wolves will come in among you and will not spare the flock. Even from your own number men will arise and distort the truth in order to draw away disciples after themselves.

The Amplified version of verse 30 reads as follows:

> Even from your own selves men will come to the front, who by saying perverse [distorted and corrupt] things will endeavor to draw away the disciples after them [to their own party].

In modern wording, ". . . will endeavor to draw away disciples to their own particular denomination or fellowship."

There were many elders but only one flock, and Paul told all the elders to watch over the entire flock. The practice of segregating little pieces of the flock and laying claims on them was also dealt with in this passage. Paul said that when he left, he knew some of the pastors would "draw away disciples after themselves." In some measure, this happens every time a pastor makes up his membership roll and tries to lock people unto himself and away from the rest of the body of Christ and away from any spiritual input from any other pastor in town.

"But if I tell my people that they are members of every church in town, they will not be faithful to this fellowship in their attendance and in their giving," moans the nervous pastor. This is a great concern to many leaders. The cry is, "Come and help us fulfill our vision." The cry should be, "Come and let us help you fulfill your vision and your calling." Apostles, prophets, evangelists, pastors, and teachers were given to the church "to prepare God's people for works of service." God imparts gifts, callings, anointing, and vision to every member of His Body. It is a vision to serve Him in some specific way, and it is the job of these leaders to help prepare God's people to fulfill these works of service. Too many pastors envision using all the sheep they can gather together to help them build up the local congregation, with little thought of building the Kingdom of God and helping fulfill the Great Commission.

The Problems of "Paper Membership"

Some of the problems of "Paper Membership" are:

- We are presuming that we know who is truly born again and therefore qualified to be **added to the number**. Only the Lord knows who is saved and can be added to the number.

- A membership list is usually a device used to receive people into a formal, on-going relationship. This seems innocent enough at first glance, but it also tends to lock them away from the rest of the Body of Christ within the city. This creates isolated factions within the city-wide church. Why do we do this and then whine because the Body of Christ is so fragmented? We need to wake up and see that we are the reason why! This is what Paul warned would happen, "Even from your own number men will arise and distort the truth in order to draw away disciples after themselves."

- Paper Membership challenges the true basis of what the Church is and how we become a part of it. The requirement for becoming a member of the local congregation is the same as the requirement for becoming a member of the Body of Christ — being born-again. We become members of that worldwide Body the instant we are born of the Spirit of God by faith in Jesus Christ. There are no other requirements. None!

- To teach that a person can be a member of the entire Body of Christ and still not be a member of your local church is to be divisive. There is only one Body, not many bodies. There are many local churches, but they are each a part of the universal Body of Christ. Therefore, if I am a member of the whole, I am automatically a member of each part. Scripture never even touches the idea of being members of an organization. It simply says, *"We are members one of another"* (Romans 12:5). That includes all believers in all places in all the world.

• A membership list is wrong because it engenders and projects the idea that, "These sheep are mine! Stay away from my sheep!" There is not one verse of Scripture that ever gives me, as a pastor, the right to say that any of God's people are *my* sheep. It is true that a pastor is a shepherd; but Jesus said, "*You feed My sheep.*" There is one Chief Shepherd, many under-shepherds, and many sheep; but only one flock. The sheep are not told to relate only to one of the under-shepherds. The sheep can receive nurture and guidance from any and all God-called shepherds, as well as from any apostle, prophet, evangelist, or teacher.

"But where will my salary come from?" cries the unbelieving under-shepherd. It will come from the hands of the Chief Shepherd for whom you labor, who promises to meet all your needs as you do the work He has called you to do. He is your paymaster. Get your eyes off the people as your source of supply and put them on Jesus whose name is Jehovah-Jireh, your Lord and Provider.

A Biblical View of Membership

At the moment he is saved, every born-again believer is added to the Church by the Lord Jesus. He instantly becomes a part of the Body of Christ, which makes him a member of every local congregation in every place wherever he may go. Every local church within the city must see itself as a vital part of the city-wide church and of the worldwide Church. There must be no special requirements for becoming a member of a local church beyond that of receiving Jesus as Lord and Savior. A church is not an organization; it is an organism, a gathering of God's people where everyone is welcome.

Pastors and leaders must never lay claim to any of God's sheep as belonging to them. They are to nurture, protect, guide, and counsel, but never to be possessive over God's inheritance. We are co-laborers together with God, but we must learn to let go of the reins and trust the Spirit of Jesus to accomplish the work of Church building, using us in whatever way He chooses.

The elders — also called shepherds, pastors, teachers, and bishops — of each locality should develop working relationships with each other so that they can more effectively watch over God's flock.

SEVEN

Saturation Church Planting

One of the leading exponents for church planting in this century was the late Dr. Donald McGavran. In a recent "Dawn Report," Jim Montgomery shares the following:

> During the last months of Mary McGavran's illness, my wife Lyn would frequently spend time with her. Donald McGavran would be there, too, disregarding his own painful cancer while taking care of his beloved Mary.
>
> "You can be sure Jim and I will continue our commitment to church growth after you're gone," Lyn said to Donald one day.
>
> "Don't call it church growth anymore," was his quick response. "Call it church multiplication." Two weeks before his death he said, "The only way we will get the job of the great commission done is to plant a church in every community in the world."

The A.D. 2000 Movement

In the closing years of the Twentieth Century a movement called Project 2000 was born. Project 2000 has been gaining momentum all over the world. Its objective is to mobilize the Body of Christ to fulfill the Great Commission by A.D. 2000 or soon after. It is a vision that is being adopted by churches, missionary organizations, and denominations all over the world. There is more interest today in missions, world evangelization, and church planting than ever before in history. Just as Jesus predicted, His Church is irresistibly penetrating all the earth. We're getting closer to the time when truly *"the earth will be filled with the knowledge of the Lord"* (Habakkuk 2:14).

Churches in Every Neighborhood

Jesus commanded the Church to go into all the world and disciple all nations. According to mission strategists, there are about 24,000 nations (ethnic groups). It is also commonly agreed among church leaders that the only way to disciple a nation is to plant churches within that nation. It is further agreed that it will take more than a few churches to disciple a nation. It will require a strategy that envisions saturation church planting, which means planting churches in every neighborhood of 500 to 1000 people. This vision for saturation church planting is not only for developing nations, but also for all nations including Europe, Latin America, and the United States.

The Field is the World

There is no church that is reaching all the unsaved in any city or even any neighborhood. We need all the help we can get to reach out to those in need. If a house church movement will speed up the evangelization of my city, I want to start as many house churches as I can and see that they multiply. I am also committed to encouraging any other pastor who loves and exalts Jesus in his efforts to multiply congregations within my city or any other city.

The Death of Pride and Greed

How important is it to us to have a large congregation with large offerings and beautiful buildings? We have been led to believe that these are sure signs of success in the ministry, so we strive to build up a large congregation. We want to be a success in the eyes of our peers, our people, our leaders, and in our own eyes. Consequently, we get caught in this web of deception. This produces a spirit of greed, selfishness, pride, and possessiveness. In this climate there is no thought of sending anyone out to the mission field or down the street to start another congregation. The only thought that meets with approval in such churches is something that will add more people to that congregation. The Spirit of God is grieved in such churches. We praise God that not all large churches have such questionable motivation!

Develop Unpaid Leaders from Among the People

Some are concerned that a strategy for multiplying house churches will lead to inept, unqualified leaders. Jesus did not go to the Levites or to the religious institutions of His day to pick the men He would use to lead out in building His Church. He chose fishermen and ordinary men whom He empowered with the Holy Spirit. God loves to use little things and weak things.

> For you see your calling, brethren, how that not many wise men after the flesh, not many mighty, not many noble, are called; But God has chosen the foolish things of the world to confound the wise; and God has chosen the weak things of the world to confound the things which are mighty; And base things of the world, and things which are despised, has God chosen, yea and things which are not, to bring to naught things that are, That no flesh should glory in His presence (1 Corinthians 1:26-29).

In every movement that has had worldwide significance in the spread of the gospel throughout the history of the Church, ordinary men and women have had a leading roll. John Wesley was a man of great learning with years of education and religious training. But as the leader of one of the greatest revival and church planting movements of history, he did not go to the established schools of religious training to find his pastors and leaders. He said,

> Give me twelve men who love Jesus with all their hearts and who do not fear men or devils, and I care not one whit whether they be clergy or laity. With these men I will change the world.

And that is just what Mr. Wesley did! To preach the gospel in the open air in Wesley's day was the height of sacrilege and a serious affront to the established church. It was unthinkable in the Church of England to stand outside of the walls of the holy sanctuaries to proclaim the sacred Word of God. The Wesley brothers and George Whitefield suffered years of persecution for breaking the long-standing traditions of the established church, but this did not deter them. They knew the Scriptures and were convinced that if Jesus could do such things it was acceptable for them to do the same.

Drawing again from Dr. McGavran's *Understanding Church Growth*, under the subtitle "Eight Keys to Church Growth," he writes:

> Develop unpaid lay leaders. Laymen have played a great part in urban expansions of the church. One secret of growth in the cities of Latin America has been that, from the beginning, unpaid common men led the congregations, which therefore appeared to the masses to be truly Chilean or Brazilian affairs. In any land, when laborers, mechanics, clerks, or truck drivers teach the Bible, lead in prayer, tell what God has done for them, or exhort the brethren, the Christian religion looks and sounds natural to ordinary men. Whatever unpaid laymen, earning their living as others do, subject to the same hazards and bound by the same work schedules, lack in correctness of Bible teaching or beauty of prayers, they more than make up for by their intimate contact with their own people. No paid worker from the outside and

certainly no missionary from abroad can know as much about a neighborhood as someone who has dozens of relatives and intimates all about him. True, on new ground the outsider has to start new expansions. No one else can. But the sooner he turns the churches over to local men the better.

In his book *Breaking the Stained Glass Barrier*, David Womack, an Assemblies of God missionary, wrote,

> There is only one way the Great Commission can be fulfilled, and that is by establishing gospel-preaching congregations in every community on the face of the earth.

Roger Greenway, a specialist in reaching cities for the Lord, says in *Discipling the City*,

> The church's evangelistic task demands that every barrio, apartment building, and neighborhood have a church faithful to God's Word established in it.

Churches by the Millions

When I first read the book by Jim Montgomery, *Dawn 2000*, with a subtitle that I could hardly believe, "Seven Million Churches To Go," I thought to myself, "How could anyone even dare to think in terms of planting millions of churches?" I hadn't read long before I knew that I could also believe with Jim Montgomery for seven million churches to be planted throughout the world. We are in the leading edge of the strongest missionary movement in history. There is more interest in reaching every tongue, tribe and nation now than there ever has been since Jesus died, rose again, and ascended to the Father.

Throughout the whole world, let us finish the task, preach the gospel to every creature, disciple all the nations, and bring Christ back to reign in righteousness as the kingdoms of this world become the Kingdom of our God.

The Christian movement is gaining momentum daily. The rock that was cut out of the mountain without hands and came crashing down the mountain to smite the feet of the statue in the vision of the prophet Daniel is growing larger each day! It has already crashed into the feet of this world's system and will soon grow into a mountain that will cover the earth with the knowledge of the Lord as the waters cover the sea.

The key to the fulfillment of the Great Commission is to plant churches. The plan that is attracting the attention of many mission strategists these days is to plant a church in every community of 500 to 1000 people — that's saturation church planting. We will have to discard our stained-glass concept of church. We can no longer think of church as buildings. We must begin to think of church as people. And that means people coming together in the name of Jesus in homes, shops, offices, factories, stores, schools, mortuaries, parks, jails, prisons, hospitals, deserted buildings, street corners, halls, women's clubs, and service clubs — as well as in dedicated church buildings.

The House Church Pastor

> And His gifts were that some should be apostles, some prophets, some evangelists, some pastors and teachers, to equip the saints for the work of ministry (Ephesians 4:11-12).

The pastor is part of the team to bring the body up to strength to be able to minister to itself. Actually it is the body that has the job of bringing itself to maturity. The apostle, prophet, evangelist, pastor, and teacher are to equip the body unto,

> . . . the building up of the Body of Christ, until we all attain to the unity of the faith and of the knowledge of the Son of God to mature manhood, to the measure of the stature of the fullness of Christ . . . from whom the whole body, joined and knit together by every joint by which it is supplied, when each part is working properly, makes bodily growth and upbuilds itself in love.

The True and the False

We cannot allow the enemy to achieve so great a victory as to deny the church the ministry of the truly God-called and anointed pastor. We cannot disqualify all pastors because some have been self-centered, self-serving, and abusive in their position of spiritual authority. Where there is the counterfeit, there is always the genuine and the authentic. We have no more right to cancel out the ministry of pastor than we do to cancel out the ministry of prophet, apostle, or evangelist. They are all ordained of God to function for the upbuilding of the Church.

It is the Body that Builds Up the Body

The work of the apostle, prophet, evangelist, pastor, and teacher is to equip the body to minister to itself and to bring itself up to maturity. If we get this wrong and try to put the work of the body onto the equippers, we will never see the Body of Christ grow to the "measure of the stature of the fullness of Christ." The Phillips translation of Ephesians 4:16 says,

> The whole body, as a harmonious structure knit together by the joints with which it is provided, grows by the proper functioning of individual parts, and so builds itself up in love.

The Living Bible says,

> The whole body is fitted together perfectly, and each part in its own special way helps the other parts, so that the whole body is healthy and growing and full of love.

The Purpose of Leaders in the Church

For centuries, church leaders have been trying to do the work that only the body can do, and the body has not been functioning to bring itself up to the measure of the stature of the fullness of Christ. The effectual working of every part of the body is the only way it can be done, but the body must be equipped by the leaders that God has placed in the church for that purpose.

The apostle, prophet, evangelist, pastor, and teacher are valid leadership, sent by the Lord as gifts to His church for a very specific purpose — to equip the church to build itself up. It is just as bad for the Body not to allow the leaders to function as it is for the leaders not to allow the Body to function. The Body of Christ will only come into strength if every part is properly functioning, and that includes pastors and leaders.

The Parable of the Two Motors

In every car there are two motors — one runs on gasoline and the other on electricity. The gasoline motor is huge in comparison to the electric motor; but it is the tiny little electric motor that is designed to start the gasoline motor, and the gasoline motor is designed to provide the power to move the car. As soon as the big motor engages, the little motor disengages. If it did not, it would burn out in a matter of minutes.

The apostle, prophet, evangelist, pastor, and teacher are servants to the Body of Christ to act as initiators (starters) to get the Body functioning. Just as the starter motor disengages as soon as the big motor starts, so it is with the wise leader. If he stays engaged, he will burn out, just as a starter motor would do if it did not disengage after starting the big motor.

As long as the little starter motor is trying to move the car by the power of a single battery, the car will never function as it was designed to function. It is only the 350 horsepower motor that has been designed to move the car, and it is only the Body of Christ that has been designed to build up the Body unto the measure of the fullness of Christ. Only as the Body of Christ is released to minister to itself will it ever attain unto the fullness of maturity in Christ.

God's Gifts are Good Gifts

The word of God calls these men and their function in the church *gifts*. They are gifts sent from God. All of God's gifts are good. None of them are bad. If some of them have been corrupted, that is not the fault of the Giver. Let us believe God for a restoration in these days of godly pastors, evangelists, teachers, apostles, and prophets.

Pastoral Oversight

Apparently the house churches that Paul planted in Derbe, Iconium, Antioch, and Lystra functioned before he appointed elders (cf. Acts 13 and Acts 14). The more we release the Body of Christ to do what it was designed to do, the sooner we will see the explosive growth that we read about in the New Testament. A shepherd does not have to hover over the shoulder of each sheep to make sure he is eating. He simply makes sure that the sheep are in a good place where there is plenty to eat, and he lets them function on their own. He is there when needed to take care of special problems, but does not deem it necessary to be involved in everything the sheep are doing.

On the other hand, Jesus himself gave us a picture of what it is like when sheep have no shepherd.

> And seeing the multitudes, He felt compassion for them, because they were distressed and downcast like sheep without a shepherd (Matthew 9:36).

Sheep without a shepherd become distressed and downcast. When I began to see these things, I started praying about how to function as a pastor should function. I honestly did not know how far to back off in order to allow the Body to function. "Lord," I prayed, "give me wisdom in this matter." The Lord heard my prayer and gave me three little parables that have helped me to understand my role as a pastor. I have already shared the one about the two motors.

The Parable of the Tomato Plant

While eating lunch one day with my wife, I remarked how tasty the tomatoes were that we had raised out on our patio. "The tomatoes in the super markets are nothing like these." I said, "These are so much more delicious!"

Just as I spoke those words, I heard the Lord say, "How much did you do to bring forth those tomatoes?"

"Not very much," I thought to myself. "I just prepared the soil in a clay pot, bought the tomato plants, put the roots under the soil, and watered them from time to time. A couple of times I put some plant food in the water."

"That's how it is with the church," the Lord said. "You didn't have to do very much to enable those tomato plants to do their thing. You just had to set the conditions for growth, and they grew. It is programmed into their nature to work day and night to bring forth those beautiful, red, juicy, delicious tomatoes. So it is with the Church. It is organic, and if you will just work with Me to set the conditions, the Church will grow of its own accord. It will produce good fruit for I have ordained it to be so."

The Parable of the Fire on the Beach

I was down on the beach early in the morning as was my custom when we lived in Laguna Beach, California. I used to go down almost every morning with a beach chair, some matches and old newspapers, some books, and my Bible. There was always plenty of driftwood that I could gather off the beach to build my fire. On this particular morning, I built my fire as usual, and after an hour or so, I took a walk on the beach. When I returned the fire had died down. I found some more wood and stoked the hot coals, then put the wood on the coals. In less than a minute I had a good fire going again. I sat down to enjoy the fire a little longer before going up to the house for breakfast.

As I sat looking into the fire, the Lord spoke to me. "That's how the church is. Your work is like watching over this fire. You cannot make a fire burn. You can only set the conditions for a fire to burn. Then when it dies down, you can rekindle the flames as you see the need. You cannot bring the fire of My Spirit, but you can help set the stage for His coming. I want you to enjoy overseeing the church. All you have to do is just be ready to stir the coals and put on more wood. The fire burns of its own accord. This is the work of a pastor."

Qualifications of Elders

In Ephesians 20:28-30 Paul is addressing all the elders of Ephesus. He says,

> Guard yourselves and all the flock [one flock] of which the Holy Spirit has made you overseers [Bishops]. Be shepherds [pastors] of the church of God, which He bought with His blood. I know that after I leave, savage wolves will come in among you and will not spare the flock. Even from your own number men will arise and distort the truth in order to draw away disciples after them.

This makes it clear that an elder is a bishop and a pastor. They are one and the same. The qualifications of an elder are listed in two places in the New Testament — 1 Timothy 3:1-7, and Titus 1:5-9.

> Here is a noteworthy saying: If anyone sets his heart on being an overseer, he desires a noble task. Now the overseer must be above reproach, the husband of but one wife, temperate, self-controlled, respectable, hospitable, able to teach, not given to much wine, not violent but gentle, not quarrelsome, not a lover of money. He must manage his own family well and see that his children obey him with proper respect. (If anyone does not know how to manage his own family, how can he take care of God's church?) He must not be a recent convert, or he may become conceited and fall under the same judgment as the devil. He must also have a good reputation with outsiders, so that he will not fall into disgrace and into the devil's trap (1 Timothy 3:1-7).

> The reason I left you in Crete was that you might straighten out what was left unfinished and appoint elders in every town, as I directed you. An elder must be blameless, the husband of but one wife, a man whose children believe and are not open to the charge of being wild and disobedient. Since an overseer is entrusted with God's work, he must be blameless-not overbearing, not quick-tempered, not given to much wine, not violent, not pursuing dishonest gain. Rather he must be hospitable, one who loves what is good, who is self-controlled, upright, holy and disciplined. He must hold firmly to the trustworthy message as it has been taught, so that he can encourage others by sound doctrine and refute those who oppose it (Titus 1:5-9).

In both passages quoted above there is no mention of academic achievement required to become an elder. All of the important qualities of a leader have to do with a man's walk with Jesus. Here they are in one long list taken from both passages above:

- Blameless

- One wife

- Believing, obedient children

- Hospitable

- Lover of the good

- Self-controlled

- Holy

- Disciplined

- Able to teach

- Temperate

- Respectable

- Not given to much wine

- Not violent

• Not quarrelsome

• Not a lover of money

• Manages his own household well

• Mature in the things of the Lord

• Having a good reputation

That's it! These are simply the qualities of a spiritual man; a man fully consecrated to Jesus Christ. The reason we have to put our leaders through such rigorous training in so many different fields of knowledge is that we have moved away from simplicity. Church is no longer a simple gathering of believers for mutual edification and worship. It is big business.

But God is calling us back to simplicity. And He is also calling us to recognize the men and women that He is bringing into leadership. If we will simplify our concept of church we will automatically simplify our requirements for leadership.

EIGHT

A Wheel
or a Vine?

Think of a wheel, laying on the ground with spokes going out in all directions from a hub at the center. Now, think of a vine growing on the ground reaching out its branches in all directions, sending down roots at intervals, and at each interval giving birth to another plant just like itself with the same potential to send out branches which send down roots at intervals.

Which of the above best describes the Saturation Church Planting strategy, the wheel or the vine? It is not a question of which one works. They both work, but one is organization and the other is organic. The traditional church is using the wheel concept, but some are beginning to see the wisdom of the vine concept of church planting.

The Wheel

The wheel concept calls for all the baby churches (cell groups) to be closely tied to and dependent upon the mother church. Normally they are not called churches. They are seen as an extension of the mother church. All the people in the little churches meet during the week so that they can attend the mother church on Sunday morning. All tithes and offerings are channeled into the mother church, and the leaders of the cell churches are not seen as pastors. From time to time, one of the cell churches are released to become a full-fledged, bona-fide church; and a pastor is appointed. This, in essence, is the wheel concept. It has been very successful in some places and has produced some very large congregations.

The Vine

The vine concept of church planting can be illustrated by the spider plant. The spider plant has long, graceful, variegated leaves resembling a miniature weeping willow tree. Out from among the leaves shoot long vines that produce smaller spider plants at intervals along the vine. The little baby spiders never get as big as the mother plant because, unlike the mother plant which has its roots potted in soil, the baby spiders are left to dangle in the air and take all their life from the mother plant. If this beautiful hanging plant is taken down from its hanging position and planted in the ground, each one of the little spider plants begin to send down their own roots into the ground. When that happens, each little baby plant begins to grow and to put down its own roots and send out vines in all directions, giving birth to an endless number of beautiful mature spider plants.

Tendencies

- The wheel tends to draw unto itself, while the vine tends to release outward.
- The wheel tends to be local, while the vine tends to be trans-local.
- The wheel tends toward addition, while the vine tends toward multiplication.
- The wheel tends to build one church, while the vine tends toward building many churches.

- The wheel tends to restrict missionary vision, while the vine tends to promote missionary vision.
- The wheel encompasses the community, while the vine encompasses the world.
- The wheel envisions cell groups, while the vine envisions churches meeting in houses.

May the Lord of the harvest give us a vision for church planting that will allow the fullest freedom of the life of the church to express itself without restrictions.

NINE

One Step
to Unity

Someone may ask, "But won't all these little house churches scattered throughout a city cause division and disunity in the Body of Christ within the city?" Little churches cause no more division than big ones. Very large churches and very small churches have the same challenge when it comes to unity.

Organizational Unity or Spiritual Unity

What is the difference between spiritual unity and organizational unity? We are all members of the same body; therefore, we are one, spiritually. You may not be a member of my organization; but if you belong to Jesus, you belong to me, and I belong to you. All that belongs to the Father and to the Son belongs to all the children of God everywhere. We are members of His flesh and of His bones, and we are members one of another.

One City, One Church

Paul never wrote to the *churches* of any city. He always wrote to *the church* of that particular city. There is only one church in each city, or locality. He writes to the *church* in Rome, Corinth, Ephesus, etc. But he writes to the *churches* in Galatia, the *churches* in Asia, etc., because these were provinces and not cities. There is only one church in each locality, though there may be scores or even hundreds of churches that meet in Jesus' name within that locality. The many smaller gatherings make up the one church in that city. Just as all the churches in all the cities in the world make up the Body of Christ — the Church Universal — so all the churches (congregations) within a locality make up the church in that city.

Keep the Unity

In Ephesians 4:3-6 we read,

> Make every effort to keep the unity of the Spirit through the bond of peace. There is one body and one Spirit . . . one Lord, one faith, one baptism: one God and Father of all who is over all and through all and in all.

In the above passage Paul did not say, "Establish the unity of the Spirit." He said, ". . . keep the unity of the Spirit," as if it were something that already existed. He speaks here as if unity were something that comes automatically as a part of the package. We are born-again into unity because, "There is one Body, one Spirit, one Lord, one Father, one God." Our part is simply an acknowledgement that we are already one. To fulfill the command to keep the unity of the Spirit in the bond of peace is to keep something that we already have, for you cannot keep what you do not yet have. This unity is not external structures. It is neither born in external ties nor maintained by external ties. It is born in the Spirit and in the heart. It is an interior attitude. It is an attitude toward people — the people of God.

Unity with Diversity

We can have all the diversity we want to have as far as organizations, denominations and fellowships are concerned and still have unity in the Spirit. We are not held together by formal membership. We are held together by the unity of the Spirit in the bond of peace. On the other hand, you can have one giant organization that includes every Christian on earth and still have no real unity in the Spirit, though you may have organizational oneness.

The bond in Ephesians 3:4-6 speaks of something that ties together, like a rope or belt. That bond is peace. The opposite of peace is strife or war. If you have an attitude of love and acceptance toward your brothers and sisters in other churches, you are *keeping the unity* with them. You are not creating it. You are keeping it alive in your own spirit, and that is where unity exists. It works itself out in different ways, but it exists in the spirit by means of the Holy Spirit. Conversely, if you have an attitude of strife, divisiveness, or sectarianism, you are not keeping the unity of the Spirit through the bond of peace. The *us and them* mentality is rampant within the Body of Christ, and it **must** be dealt with!

An Inward Step

The one and only step to unity, then, is found in Romans 14:1 and 15:7,

> Accept those whose faith is weak without passing judgment on disputable matters . . . Accept one another, then, just as Christ accepted you.

The word *accept* means to welcome, embrace, receive; to acknowledge kinship, to confess and declare the fact that we are one because by the new birth we have all been born into the same spiritual family. We are all brothers and sisters because Jesus is our Savior, and God is our Father. Just as Jesus received us with all our brokenness, faults, and immaturity, so let us receive one another.

Take the Step Now

This one step to unity can be taken right where you are this very moment. You can lift your heart to the Lord right now and pray: "Father, in the name of Jesus Christ my Lord, I do acknowledge that I am a member of your spiritual Body, the Church in this city, and throughout the world. I do accept and receive every one of your children as my brother or sister because you are our Father. It doesn't matter where they live. It doesn't matter what race they are, what peculiar beliefs or practices they may have, or whether they are post, pre, or a-millennialist. It doesn't matter if they baptize by sprinkling, pouring, or by immersion, whether they are Arminianists or Calvinists. It doesn't matter if they go to church on Saturday, Sunday, Monday or Tuesday; whether they are Catholic, Protestant, Orthodox or Jew. I don't care if they are Baptist, Methodist, Presbyterian or Foursquare. I do now declare in the name of Jesus Christ the Lord, the Son of God Almighty, that I am one with every other born-again believer that lives, that has lived, or ever will live in time and in eternity. I will accept them; I will receive them. I will love them and support them. I will pray for them. As you direct me, Lord, I will co-labor with them, and I will endeavor to keep this unity of the Spirit through the bond of peace. Amen."

When you sincerely pray such a prayer, you have taken the one step to unity. "But what about doctrinal unity? How can we walk together unless we are agreed?" God is not directing us all to walk in the same direction. We are told in Ephesians 4:12 that we are to keep this unity of the Spirit "until we all come into the unity of the faith." We can have spiritual unity while we are coming into doctrinal unity.

One Central Truth

There is only one central truth around which we can all declare our unity, and that truth is not a teaching nor a concept nor a principle nor a doctrine. It is not a church, or a denomination, or a movement. That truth is a Person. Jesus is the truth. He said, *"I am the Way, the Truth, and the Life"* (John 14:6). When we come to Him, He gives us life. We are born again! When the Philippian jailer asked Paul and Silas, "Sirs, what must I do to be saved?" they did not tell him to believe their doctrine and join their organization. They said, "Believe on the Lord Jesus Christ, and you will be saved." We believe on a Person and are born into the kingdom of light. When we are joined to Jesus, we are joined to one another. We are one in Him. He who has Jesus has life. He who does not have Jesus does not have life. We are saved, not by embracing a doctrinal position, but by receiving Jesus Christ Himself.

Receive One Another

In every church, whether it is a house church or a traditional church, we must accept every other believer as members of the same Body without regard to denominational affiliation. God may lead us at times to cooperate in larger projects, but the most powerful expression of unity is in accepting and affirming one another in what we are already doing on many different fronts in many different places.

Many Leaders — One Army

We are all in warfare and there are many generals, lieutenants, captains, and foot soldiers; but there is only one Head — our Commander-in-Chief, Jesus Christ Himself. He said, *"I will build My Church."* And that is what He is doing. Let's make room for Him to build His Church. He has charge of every small unit of His mighty army. We may be in different divisions, in different units, on a different front; but we are still one army, one people, fighting the same war against the kingdom of darkness. Let us affirm and support one another in our various places of service without thinking that we are separated just because we're not all in the same place doing the same things at the same time under the same banner.

Many Tribes — One Nation

There were twelve tribes in Israel, each with its own territory, genealogy, leaders, and banner. But, they were still one people, Israel. We may be made up of hundreds, or even thousands of denominations, organizations and churches, but we are one people, the people of God. We do not have to be physically together doing the same things under the same flag in order to be one. We are already one; so let us boldly proclaim our unity and go about our business of extending His kingdom while affirming, accepting and receiving one another. That is "keeping the unity of the Spirit through the bond of peace."

TEN

What Do You Do in a House Church?

It is significant that neither Paul nor Jesus Himself gave specific instructions to us as to exactly what should be done when we congregate as a church. Jesus' words were very simple in Matthew 18:20, "For where two or three are gathered together in my name, there am I in the midst of them." He did not say they had to be doing certain things in order for Him to be in the midst — just gathered together in His name. The apostle Paul gave us a little insight into the nature of early church gatherings in 1 Corinthians 14:26,

> What shall we say brothers? When you come together, everyone has a hymn, or a word of instruction, a revelation, a tongue or an interpretation. All of these things must be done for the strengthening of the church.

Church meetings in those days were not speaker-oriented. It was an open meeting where each person was to contribute for the benefit of the whole body. The exercise of spiritual gifts was encouraged so that all were blessed and edified. We can glean from the book of Acts and the Epistles some of the essential elements of the meetings in the First Century Church.

Praise and Prayer

It is always good to begin each meeting with an extended time of praise and worship intermittent with spontaneous prayers. Sometimes this will be done just between our soul and God, but at times He will impress us to pray out loud so that all may be edified. Musicians add dimension to the praise time, but they are not absolutely essential. CD's and cassettes are working very well in many groups. Some of the most powerful of all praise can certainly come forth without any instruments or back-up music. Just singing to the Lord from the heart without instruments is pure praise and worship.

We seem to have come to the place in our day that we are praising our praise and worshiping our worship. If it does not give us goose bumps, we feel that we have not entered the Holy of Holies. We are not performing for our own enjoyment, but for the Lord's — and He is perfectly content with all praise as long as it comes from a sincere heart. There will be times when the Holy Spirit will lead you to do nothing more than praise the Lord. Be open to His leading. All things flow out from prayer, praise, and worship.

Sharing

This is a time for sharing ministry gifts according to 1 Corinthians 14:26. In an open meeting, the leader directs and encourages the group to share testimonies, experiences, prayer requests, brief teachings, revelations, praise reports, etc. Be watchful that the extroverts do not dominate the sharing time. Draw out the quiet ones by asking questions. It is sometimes necessary to exhort in the beginning of the sharing time that the quiet ones "step out of the boat," put down their fear of man, and give a word of testimony for the Lord. It is just as necessary to encourage those more talkative ones to hold back and give others the opportunity to speak.

Communion

Let someone explain the meaning of communion, then let the brothers and sisters partake of the body and blood of our Lord with understanding and faith. This is a time to examine ourselves and repent of any sin that the Lord might reveal to us as we wait on Him. Before serving the bread and the cup is a good time to invite those who do not know Christ to pray and receive Him. Many are ready to receive Jesus if we will only give a brief explanation of the gospel and lead the congregation in a prayer of receiving Christ. Many are led to Christ in this way. Those who receive Christ as Savior should receive water baptism immediately. The example of the early church in the book of Acts was always to baptize new converts on the same day they received Jesus.

Ministry

Be open to minister to one another through prophetic ministry, the laying on of hands, praying for the sick, releasing those who are bound by harassing spirits, ministering the filling of the Holy Spirit, etc. Let all the gifts of the Spirit flow freely for the edification of all according to 1 Corinthians 14. Take care not to let the "super minister" dominate during this time. Let the Body of Christ minister to itself in love.

Discussion Bible Study

Because of the open church format, the Holy Spirit is teaching throughout the service using various ones who participate. Over the centuries, the sermon (or teaching time) has enlarged more and more almost to the exclusion of group participation. This has led to a spectator type of service in which one person uses his gifts while the rest watch, listen, and receive (and sometimes sleep!). The discussion Bible study format tends to rectify this error and bring out the gifts of the entire body to the building up of itself. The Holy Spirit will guide in each meeting as to specifics. Do not make it a program. The following are important elements of a house church, or any church for that matter: praise, worship, prayer, sharing, teaching God's Word, encouraging the release of spiritual gifts, water baptism, the baptism in the Holy Spirit, communion, evangelism, and personal ministry to one another. These are some of the things that Jesus was talking about when He said, ". . . *teaching them to observe all things whatsoever I have commanded you, and lo, I am with you even to the end of the age.*"

ELEVEN

How to Start a House Church

When we ask the question "How do you start a house church?" we are really asking the question, "How do you start a church?" There is no such term used in the New Testament as *house church*. It does say, "Give my greetings to Nympha and the church in her house." It does not say, ". . . the house church in her house." A church that meets in a house is a church! The day will come when we will drop the term *house church* and call all the gatherings of the Saints *church*.

Safeway and Circle K

We tremble when we think of starting a church! We see it as a monumental task because we are thinking in terms of a traditional church. We praise the Lord for all the large churches who are lifting up Jesus as Lord and Savior, but in the average city in the U.S.A. more than fifty percent of the population do not attend any church. The number is even less in other countries. There is still room for many more churches in every city in the world, both big churches and small churches. We have huge supermarkets in every city, but we also have small convenience stores. Both do the same thing — they dispense food. The large markets do not meet the total needs of the populace any more than the large churches meet the total needs of the people. House churches do not compete with the larger ones. They are allies in the battle against the kingdom of darkness and in the work of fulfilling the Great Commission.

Bring on the Tanks!

I will always remember what my friend Hobart Vann used to say as he recounted some of his experiences in World War II. The war was ending, and the Allies were liberating France and Italy from German occupation. In approaching a city they would pull their tanks up to high ground overlooking the city. Soon another tank would pull up alongside theirs, then another, and still another — until there were scores of those powerful tanks poised to advance upon the city.

Hobart said,

> Bob, I never once opened the hatch on our tank and waved all the other tanks off shouting, "Hey, you guys, get away from here! This is our turf! We will take this city without your help! Stop intruding into our territory! We can take this one all by ourselves!" We were glad that we were not going in alone to liberate that city. Every one of those tanks looked beautiful to us! The rumble of their engines was music to our ears. We would have been happy to have had twice as many tanks as we had.

In like manner none of us can say, "Hey, you guys! Don't start another church in this town. We are reaching everyone in this town already!" The fastest way to evangelize a city is to start new churches. So why should I be upset if someone starts another church — be it a church that meets in a house or one that meets in a temple?

Saturation Church Planting and the House Church

If we are going to saturate cities and nations with churches we will have to begin to think in terms of starting churches in houses. The fastest church growth in history is taking place in China through saturation church planting directed by the Holy Spirit. This is not a theory but is a practical reality and stands as a testimony to the Church worldwide as to the effectiveness of massive church planting.

To Start a Church in a House

The following are matters to consider in starting a church in a house. You may implement some of them or all of them. The important thing is to do what the Holy Spirit tells you to do in your own particular situation.

• Pray and Get Others to Pray

The key to all success in the kingdom of God is prayer. But it is not enough just to pray. Get others to pray with you. Find someone who shares the vision and pray with him for God's direction as to how to proceed.

• Work with the Apostle, Prophet, Evangelist, Pastor, and Teacher

Acts 8:1 and 11:19-26 says,

> And on that day a great persecution arose against the Church in Jerusalem; and they were all scattered throughout the regions of Judea and Samaria, except the apostles . . .

> So then those who were scattered because of the persecution that arose in connection with Stephen made their way to Phoenicia and Cyprus and Antioch, speaking the word to no one except to Jews alone. But there were some of them, men of Cyprus and Cyrene, who came to Antioch and began speaking to the Greeks also, preaching the Lord Jesus. And the hand of the Lord was with them, and a large number who believed turned to the Lord. And the news about them reached the ears of the church at Jerusalem, and they sent Barnabas off to Antioch. Then

when he had come and witnessed the grace of God, he
rejoiced and began to encourage them all with resolute
heart to remain true to the Lord; for he was a good man,
and full of the Holy Spirit and of faith. And considerable
numbers were brought to the Lord. And he left for Tarsus
to look for Saul; and when he had found him, he brought
him to Antioch. And it came about that for an entire year
they met with the church, and taught considerable
numbers; and the disciples were called Christians in
Antioch.

It was not the Apostles who planted the church in the city
of Antioch. It was the Christians who were scattered by the
persecution who started the church in that city. The Apostles
all remained in Jerusalem (see Acts 8:1). When they heard
what was happening in Antioch they sent Barnabas to help
give it encouragement and strength.

The phenomenal house church movement in China
shows that anyone who loves and serves the Lord Jesus can
start churches. But we need apostolic oversight and all the
gifts to the church mentioned in the fourth chapter of
Ephesians to bring it to perfection, so that it can minister to
itself and bring itself up to maturity.

Father, show us how to strengthen the Church. Help us
as pastors and leaders not to control, stifle, manipulate, or
suffocate the Church. Enable us to set the church free to be
all that you created the Church to be.

• Have a Simple Meal with Communion at the End

There is no one particular biblical way to meet. Some
meetings will be mostly praise and worship, some prayer,
some testimonies of God's goodness to us, some Bible study,
some ministering to one another, some teaching, etc.
However, it is central to the ongoing of the gospel of Jesus
Christ that we celebrate the Communion of the bread and the
wine often. We must give supreme importance to the
atonement.

We would be wise to celebrate the broken body and the
shed blood of Jesus every time we meet. Ask several people
to share what it means to them before taking it. Let someone
bring a brief teaching on the meaning of the Lord's Supper. It
is an excellent opportunity to lead people to the Lord.

• Start Small

Matthew 18:20 says, *"Where two or three have gathered together in My name, there I am in their midst."* The words *gathered together* could be translated *congregated.* It only takes two or three to make a congregation according to this verse. A congregation of people who bear the name of Jesus, with Jesus in the midst is church. Pray for growth to come, but do not become discouraged if the church is small. It will grow, and in time you will send out two or three couples to start another congregation in another section of the city or in a town nearby.

• Be Active in Several House Churches

You can be involved in more than one house church. Some of the saints are seeing this and are feeling free to extend themselves out into the Body of Christ to help in more than one place. Also, one pastor can oversee more than one house church.

• Be Free to Meet Whenever and Wherever

Meet Sunday morning, Saturday night, or any time. Gather in the same house all the time or meet in different houses from time to time. Have long or short meetings. It is okay to go on a campout together and have a praise meeting as a part of the outing. Church is people coming together in the name of Jesus. It is not a *service.*

• Do Not Make Up a Membership List

For the reasons cited above, do not make some people members and some non-members. They will never be your sheep anyway. They all belong to Jesus if they have been born-again. If they have not, then you may have the high privilege of leading them to the Lord. Until then, they are as welcome to attend your meetings as anyone.

• Receive All Who Come

Some who come to your house church will not be members of another fellowship. Since we do not have a membership list, this is no problem. We are not trying to dislodge anyone from anything the Lord is telling them to do; neither shall we tell them they cannot come to our meetings. We must receive all who come to us just as every other church in town should receive all who come to their meetings.

• Do Not Write a Constitution and By-Laws

The New Testament is our constitution and by-laws. It is totally sufficient. We need not formulate some other document to give us direction as a church. A New Testament church should take its direction from the pages of the New Testament under the guidance of the Holy Spirit. Many churches are opting to function outside the boundaries of the non-profit religious organization for various reasons. Let the Lord lead you in this matter. The only advantage a federal non-profit status gives is a deduction on our income tax for offerings given to the church. The day is coming when we will simply give to the Lord and expect no advantage on tax day. We are not against taking advantage of this tax break. Use it if the Lord gives you peace about it. But the day may come when the disadvantages of being a registered, non-profit, religious organization will outweigh the advantages.

• Don't Throw Rocks at the *Traditional Church*

We are a part of the traditional church because we are a part of the city-wide church. The problems of the church are our problems because we are the Church. Let's not fall into the snare into which the early Christians in Corinth fell. In 1 Corinthians 1:10-13 Paul says,

> I appeal to you, brothers, in the name of our Lord Jesus Christ, that all of you agree with one another so that there may be no divisions among you and that you may be perfectly united in mind and thought. My brothers, some from Chloe's household have informed me that there are quarrels among you. What I mean is this: One of you says, "I follow Paul"; another, "I follow Apollos"; another, "I follow Cephas"; still another, "I follow Christ." Is Christ divided? Was Paul crucified for you? Were you baptized into the name of Paul? (NIV)

It is not difficult to understand that it would be wrong to say, "I am of Paul, or I am of Apollos, or I am of Cephas." But how could it be wrong to say, "I am of Christ"? It is wrong to say "I am of Christ" when you mean "I am not of you because I am of Christ." This attitude comes from a sectarian or divisive spirit. Therefore it is wrong to say, "I am of the house church movement; I am not of the traditional church." That is a bad spirit that comes from an *us and them* mentality. We are one if we have the same Savior and the same Father in heaven! Therefore we must think and speak so that we are embracing our unity and not disclaiming it.

• Meet Regularly

I believe in casual church such as the two disciples had on the road to Emmaus when Christ suddenly was "in the midst." We have more church meetings than we think we have because of these casual times with other believers, but if we are going to do church planting we need to appoint regular meeting times. The Lord may lead you to change the time and place occasionally, but there should be some regularity to the meetings.

• Why Should We Meet?

For many, church has become a chore — something we have to do — and we find ourselves glad when it is over for another week.

Why meet? This is a valid question and deserves a thoughtful answer. Hebrews 10:24-25 tells us that we must not give up meeting together as some are in the habit of doing but to encourage one another, "and all the more as you see the day approaching." We must come together if we are to have strength for the days ahead. It does not have to be a large gathering for us to receive all we need to receive and impart all we need to impart. Even with a very small gathering of two or three, the dynamic of church will engage, and we will all be helped and blessed. We should not seek to be small, but we must be content if we are small.

Why meet? Togetherness is a source of strength. One other brother or sister can increase my strength by one thousand percent. In the spirit world we must move as a team. We all have blind spots. The only way we can walk in safety is to walk in plurality. Yes, we really do need one another! *"One shall chase a thousand, and two shall put ten thousand to flight"* (Deuteronomy 32:30).

Why meet? Jesus died for you and me individually, but many places in the Bible tell us that He died for the Church. *"He loved the Church and gave Himself for it,"* according to Ephesians 5:25. How can we say we love Jesus if we do not love what He loves? We must love the Church because Jesus loves the Church. If we are finding it hard to relate to the organized church, the institutional church, the traditional church, the denominational church, the problematic church, the ugly church — just remember that Jesus still relates to it, and He promised never to leave it nor forsake it. We must have the same attitude toward the Church (all of it) as our Lord has.

Why meet? To experience "Jesus in the midst." He said, *"For where two or three are gathered in my name, I am in the midst of them."* He is not in the midst of me. He lives *within* me. He is only in the midst of two or three or more of us as we get together in His name. That is a totally different experience than Jesus within. There are certain things that can only happen when Jesus is in the midst — and if we never gather in His name, they will never happen.

Why meet? There is a specific promise that "If any two of you agree as touching anything they shall ask, it shall be done for them by My Father in heaven." We can only see that promise fulfilled as we gather with at least one other Christian.

Why meet? To take Communion in company with others as His word reveals. Jesus said, *"Eat this bread and drink this cup in remembrance of Me."* He is to be remembered in the presence of His people. While it is not wrong to take the cup and the bread alone as unto the Lord, the only example we have in the New Testament is that they took it in company with other saints.

Why meet? The Apostle James tells us that we should *"confess our sins one to another and pray for another that we may be healed."* We see this phrase *one another* coming up again and again throughout the New Testament. There is no way we can avoid the clear conclusion that we are part of a Body.

Why meet? To glorify the name of Jesus as we worship and praise His name together and to follow the example of the early Church that met daily from house to house and in public places. By doing this they filled Jerusalem with the teachings of Christ.

Why meet? To allow the Body to minister to the Body.

These are some of the reasons why we come together in the name of Jesus. The revival movements that continue to thrive in the world today are in places where God's people gather daily or at least very frequently. Sunday gatherings alone were not the norm in the early Church, and it is not the norm where revival fires break out today. If God is moving in our midst in power, we will have no trouble meeting daily.

• Don't Be Afraid to Call it Church

Throughout the New Testament we find many words that are used in place of the word *church*, such as disciples, saints, assembly, believers, etc.

There will be times that we will call our meetings *church* and other times we will call them *fellowship, gatherings,* or *assemblies.* But when we gather in Jesus' name, we know it is *the Church which is His Body.*

• Submit to Spiritual Authority

We are all responsible to submit to God-ordained, spiritual authority wherever we find it. I sometimes hear pastors say, "He is our apostle." I remind them that this is not a scriptural term or a biblical concept. An apostle is an apostle wherever he goes, and a pastor is a pastor wherever he goes. But an apostle, prophet, evangelist, or teacher cannot function where he is not accepted nor respected. Neither can a pastor function where he is not received.

God gives us certain ones who are closer to us than others, but we must not reject anyone the Lord sends to us. We are members one of another; therefore we are all responsible to watch over one another to whatever extent our lives touch each other. We must embrace the city-wide church, but also remembering that we belong to the world-

wide Church. I will not relate to a brother who lives in my own city any differently than I do to a brother or sister from China or Korea. We are all one Body.

• Be a Center for World Missions

So many churches only seek to build up their own membership and thus become very ingrown and ineffective. We must live and move and pray in the Spirit of Jesus Christ and see the world as He saw it — in need of the gospel of the grace of God. Every church can develop a vision for the world. We can even adopt an unreached people group. In this way we can help reach every tongue and tribe and people and nation with the good news of God's love.

• Practice Generosity

The Bible is full of teaching on *the grace of giving.* Generosity is the clear teaching in both the Old and New Testaments. Below are some passages that promise blessing and prosperity to those who break the curse of poverty through their generosity.

> Honor the Lord with your wealth, with the firstfruits of all your crops; then your barns will be filled to overflowing, and your vats will brim over with new wine (Proverbs 3:9-10 NIV).

> A generous man will prosper; he who refreshes others will himself be refreshed (Proverbs 11:25 NIV).

> Give, and it will be given to you. A good measure, pressed down, shaken together and running over, will be poured into your lap. For with the measure you use, it will be measured to you (Luke 6:38 NIV).

> And everyone who has left houses or brothers or sisters or father or mother or children or fields for My sake will receive a hundred times as much and will inherit eternal life (Matthew 19:29 NIV).

... and if you spend yourselves in behalf of the hungry and satisfy the needs of the oppressed, then your light will rise in the darkness, and your night will become like the noonday. The Lord will guide you always; He will satisfy your needs in a sun-scorched land and will strengthen your frame. You will be like a well-watered garden, like a spring whose waters never fail (Isaiah 58:10-11 NIV).

I tell you the truth, anyone who gives you a cup of water in my name because you belong to Christ will certainly not lose his reward (Mark 9:41 NIV).

Almost without exception, when we read an admonition to give, it is followed by a promise of God's provision. Our most powerful weapon in times of financial distress is our generosity.

• Connect with Others in House Churches

There are several good house church letters that are available for the asking. I recommend that you get on one or more of the following mailing lists:

"Dawn," 7899 Lexington Drive, Suite 200-B, Colorado Springs, Colorado 80920.

"Robert Fitts Update," 76-6309 Haku Place, Kailua-Kona, HI 96740.

"House to House Magazine," 1019 Meredith, Austin, TX 78748.

I also recommend the following books (see Bibliography for further details):

Paul's Idea of Community, by Robert Banks

Going to Church in the First Century, by Robert Banks

The Church Comes Home, by Robert and Julia Banks

God's Simple Plan for His Church, by Nate Krupp

A Lost Secret of the Early Church, by W.J. Pethybridge

The Open Church, by James Rutz

Going to the Root, by Christian Smith

• Don't Preach to the Church

The Sunday morning sermon from a professional clergyman has no basis in the New Testament. In fact, the word *sermon* is not in the Bible. There is not even one mention in the New Testament of one pastor overseeing one congregation. Even the four times that the *church in a house* is mentioned, it does not designate it by the name of the pastor, but rather the name of the person in whose house they were gathered. In every instance in the New Testament where the word *preach* is used, it is referring to evangelizing the lost and not to edifying the believers. The word that Jesus gave was, *"Go into all the world and preach the gospel [good news] to every creature."* Preaching is for the lost; teaching is for the saved. Even the teaching is not to come solely from the pastors. According to 1 Corinthians 14:26, it can come from any of the brothers or sisters. This is good news to the true shepherd who has been laboriously hammering out a new *sermon* for every meeting. It will also mean that we will have to go before the Lord and find out what our true role is. I think we will find that we should simply set the stage for and lead the congregation into true Body ministry. Our best work is to help the people of God stir up their gifts and minister one to another. We have taken too much upon ourselves and many are withering under the strain.

• Use Interactive Bible Study

Several years ago the Lord showed us a type of Bible study that was very simple, spontaneous, unstructured, uncluttered and very effective. I call it *interactive Bible study*. Using this type of Bible study you do not need a teacher or any Bible study material. You only need a Bible and a few people who want to know what the Bible is all about. If one is present with a gift of teaching, let him/her participate as a learner and not as a teacher. It is group participation and not a lecture-type presentation.

The Scriptural basis for this type of Bible study is Colossians 4:16,

> After this letter has been read to you, see that it is also read in the church of the Laodiceans and that you in turn read the letter from Laodicea.

In interactive Bible study we simply read the Scripture, each taking turns reading a few verses, depending on how many people are present. While it is being read, everyone is invited to interrupt at any time to make a comment or ask a question. That is interactive Bible study.

Try it at home in your family worship. You will be surprised at how much conversation is generated and how much you learn as you read the Word of God together. Sometimes you may read long passages without any discussion at all. Just let the Word minister. Don't try to force discussion. Once it gets going the problem will be how to get back into reading. The work of the leader is in keeping both reading and discussion going — not just one or the other.

You won't need to dissect each word; just read it. It is amazing how much you can learn about the Bible by reading it! This reminds me of a conference we held several years ago. We had invited a prominent Bible teacher to be our speaker. At lunch I asked him to give us some hints on how to study the Bible. He smiled and said, "Sure, I'd be glad to."

After lunch he stood and said,

> Brother Fitts has asked me to give you some pointers on getting into Bible study, so here they are. Got your pens and paper? There are three of them: point one is, Read the Bible; point two is, Read the Bible; point three is, Read the Bible. That's it.

Everyone laughed. He didn't laugh. He meant business. He wasn't joking. We stopped laughing. We all got the point. He went on to explain the importance of just reading the Bible without any thought of *studying the Bible*. I have never forgotten that powerful lesson. Most believers have never read the Bible once. Actually, when you read the Bible you are studying the Bible. Reading is studying in its most basic form.

Paul admonished Timothy, *"Until I come, devote yourself to the public reading of Scripture, to preaching and to teaching"* (1 Timothy 4:13). We hear lots of preaching and teaching, but not much public reading of the Scripture. Preaching and teaching have their place, but so does the public reading of Scripture.

The Bible was Written
to Common, Ordinary People

Recently the question came to my mind, "Did the writers of the New Testament letters direct them to the pastors and leaders or were they addressed to the common people?" I immediately read the introduction to each letter that Paul wrote to find the answer to that question. I was amazed! We had just received an urgent cry from Russia for Bible study literature for the hundreds of house churches that were forming there. "Why literature?" I thought, "They already have the simplest, most powerful, life transforming literature in the whole world — the Bible." The New Testament was written to the common people. Look what I found as I read Paul's introduction to all his letters:

Paul, a servant of Christ Jesus . . . to all in Rome who are loved by God and called to be saints (Paul's Letter to the Romans).

Paul, called to be an apostle of Christ Jesus by the will of God . . . to the church of God in Corinth, together with all the saints through Achaia (Paul's Letter to the Corinthians).

Paul, an apostle . . . to the churches in Galatia (Paul's Letter to the Galatians).

Paul, an apostle...to the saints in Ephesus, the faithful in Christ Jesus (Paul's Letter to the Ephesians).

Paul and Timothy . . . to all the saints in Christ Jesus at Philippi together with the bishops and deacons (Paul's Letter to the Philippians — Note: This is the only letter that mentions the leaders of the church. But even this one is still addressed to all the saints, including, of course, the elders and deacons).

Paul, an apostle . . . to the holy and faithful brothers in Christ at Colossae (Paul's Letter to the Colossians).

> Paul, Silas and Timothy, to the church [the people of God] of the Thessalonians in God the Father and the Lord Jesus Christ (Paul's 1st and 2nd Letters to the Thessalonians).

I found that each letter was written to the people of God, not to an elite group of *clerics* who were in turn supposed to explain the meaning of the letters to the people. The letters were to be read to the people and that implied that they could understand the content of the letters. Of course, there is nothing wrong with explaining difficult passages, but the Holy Spirit can and will reveal the meaning of His Word to His people through His people. Group Bible study, especially interactive Bible study, is an excellent way to allow the Body to minister to the Body.

The Priesthood of the Believer

The following words of the Apostle Paul, show that the New Testament was written for the ordinary Christian. We are a *royal priesthood* and are not dependent upon a special priesthood to understand the Bible.

> I have become its servant [to the Church] by the commission God gave me to present to you the Word of God in its fullness — the mystery that has been kept hidden for ages and generations, but is now disclosed to the saints. To them God has chosen to make known among the Gentiles the glorious riches of this mystery . . . (Colossians 1:25-27).

Paul was able to give the Word of God directly to the people — even the deepest mysteries — because these mysteries are now disclosed (revealed) to the saints. Paul knew Christians could understand his writings, though Peter felt that some of Paul's writings were not that easy to understand.

These and other passages make it plain that it is not only safe but very practical to have a group of ordinary believers come together for Bible study with nothing more than the Bible. No commentaries, no quarterlies, no *experts* on the

Bible, no pastors, or teachers. Sound risky? Take the risk! Paul did, and he may well be the champion church planter of the ages!

Advantages of Interactive Bible Study

Interactive Bible study keeps the meeting informal. Let the gift of leadership arise, but let none assume the position of the expert in Bible knowledge.

In most countries there will be New Testaments, or at least portions of the New Testament, available to the people. The best Bible study material is the Bible itself.

Interactive Bible study does away with the idea that we need another book to explain the meaning of the Bible. God's Word speaks for itself.

Interactive Bible study avoids the expense of purchasing literature. In very poor countries that are just opening up to the gospel, this will be a great help not to have to bear the expense of printing or purchasing Bible study material. Even if there is only one Bible in the group, it can be passed around, and each one can read a passage.

Using the simple interactive Bible study method will make it easier to start house churches. The simpler, the easier.

Interactive Bible study makes us dependent on the Holy Spirit to comprehend what we are reading. The team approach gives balance and strength. What one will not see, someone else will. If the group gets off the track, God will reveal that, too (Philippians 3:15).

Interactive Bible study will put the emphasis back on the Bible itself. This will open up the Bible to each participant. Most Christians do not know what is in the Bible. They have heard and read much about the Bible, but seldom get into the Bible itself.

How to have an Interactive Bible Study

- Begin with prayer that all would be edified.
- It is not essential for all to have a Bible, since everyone one can share the same Bible
- Appoint a leader, but not a teacher.
- Read around the circle. Those who don't want to read can pass their turn on to another.
- Read without trying to provoke discussion.
- Invite interruptions for comments or questions.
- Keep on track. Discuss the passage being read.
- Do not let one person dominate the discussion.
- Be sensitive about when to conclude.
- End with a time of prayer and praise.

This is the sum of all we have said about interactive Bible study: It is simple; it is safe; and it is in line with the vision for bringing the body of Christ into the work of edifying itself. The Apostle Peter said,

> As each one has received a gift, minister it to one another, as good stewards of the manifold grace of God (1 Peter 4:10 KJV).

Plan and Pray for a Church Split

One of the most painful experiences anyone can go through is an old fashioned church split. It is painful only if you do not plan for one to happen. If we put regular church splits into our plans and our prayers, we will be gloriously happy, and everyone will be blessed when a split occurs. Every house church is born pregnant. Our vision from the very first day is that we will give birth to a baby church. Our plan is not to build, buy, or rent buildings that will hold lots of people. When we get too big to fit into an average size home, we will send out two or three families to start a new house church in a different place. The vision for Saturation

Church Planting is to have Christ's presence in every little
neighborhood in every city in every country in the world.
We have faith that the Great Commission of the Lord Jesus
Christ can literally be fulfilled.

Embrace the City-wide Church

Do not put a name on your church. It can become a tool
of the enemy to divide. Everyone wants to know what *brand*
of Christian you are. Do not condemn those who use names;
but if you avoid naming your fellowship, you will eventually
see the wisdom in it. To name is to denominate. The very
word denominate means *to name*. To denominate is to start a
denomination. Think it over. Is that what you want? Do not
put a name on your church more than what we find in the
New Testament, *"...the church that meets in the house of
Priscilla and Aquilla."* Remember, everything that belongs to
Jesus belongs to you, and if you belong to Jesus you belong
to me and I belong to you. That also applies to churches. I
am a member of every church that belongs to Jesus — and if
you are a member of the Body of Christ, you are, too. It is
okay to visit some of your brothers and sisters who attend
other churches, though they may not agree with you on all
points of doctrine. You may not be right on all your points of
doctrine either.

These are some of the matters to be considered when
starting a church in a house. Whether you call it *church* or
some other name, it is still the Body of Christ when believers
come together in Jesus' name.

TWELVE

Frequently Asked Questions

The following are frequently asked questions about house churches:

Q. Why house churches?

A. We have house churches for the following reasons:

- Our goal is not just to start a church. Our goal is to start a church planting movement. We believe this can best be done by focusing on the simplest and most reproducible form of church planting. The house church meets that need.

- We believe the house church concept is the best way to train pastors and leaders.

- The simplicity of small congregations makes it easy to multiply congregations.

- God is calling His people to break with traditionalism and professionalism and get back to simplicity.

• In most countries today it is the only way to get a church planting movement going. We cannot possibly do saturation church planting if we are thinking in terms of traditional church.

• It is the best environment for encouraging the Body to minister to the Body.

Q. **Isn't the house church the same as the cell group?**

A. The cell group concept is the wheel approach and the house church is the vine approach. (See Chapter 8, "A Wheel or A Vine.") A cell group is seen as a part of the outreach of another church whereas a house church is a church in itself and functions as a church, doing all the things that churches do, including baptizing, serving communion, marrying, burying, etc.

Q. **How can you develop a full church program in a house church?**

A. We believe that if we focus on the things mentioned in Chapter 10, "What Do You Do in a House Church?", the Lord will enable us to meet the needs of all the individuals and families who attend. The Holy Spirit is able to make us innovative in our approach to meeting needs. Some will need to attend churches with the ability to present more diverse programs. We are not in competition with other churches. We are working together with them to help fulfill the Great Commission.

Q. **What about children? Will they have special classes?**

A. Some house churches will have children's meetings separate from youth and adults. Some will all meet together. It is surprising how much little children learn just being with youth and adults, and how much adults can learn from children and youth! Each church will seek the Lord as to how to meet the needs of those who attend.

Q. How often do house churches meet?

A. Once or twice a week is common, but that is a decision to be made by the people of each church. There is nothing in the Bible that says when, where, or how often we should meet. The word most often used in the book of Acts is *daily*.

Q. Do you always meet in the same house?

A. We are held together by the bonds of relationship and not by the meeting place, so it is safe to move about. Moving around from home to home spreads the task of hospitality and blesses various neighborhoods.

Q. Where will you get pastors to lead these congregations?

A. The true qualifications for elders (pastors) are found in two places in the New Testament: Titus 1:6-9 and 1 Timothy 5:1-7. God has provided plenty of humble, teachable, godly men and women right in our churches who are capable of leading house churches. The apprentice method is the best method for training pastors and leaders. There has never been and never will be a better method.

Q. How does a house church give birth to another house church?

A. This is a part of the training of an elder. When he and his mentor feel the Lord is leading and the time is right, he is given a territory and the task of starting a new house church. In most cases he will be given at least one or two couples to help him get started. Ideally, one of the couples will be a pastor-in-training, so that from the very beginning of a new church there is vision for church planting. A very small house church can send out two or three couples each year to give birth to a new church.

Q. Are you suggesting that all churches should be house churches?

A. It is not our purpose to tear down anything that God is building. We are committed to bless and to assist all the churches in every city, large or small, denominational, non-denominational, or inter-denominational. We are simply presenting a valid expression of church that is based on the Word of God and that has proven effective both in the primitive church and in modern times. God is not calling all His people in all places to be doing the exact same thing. The Church of Jesus Christ is amazingly fluid and versatile in its many expressions when it is not circumscribed by rigid and inflexible traditions and practices.

Q. Should house churches belong to a denomination?

A. Every house church in any city belongs to the Church — the Body of Christ — in that city, first and foremost. A house church may belong to a denomination, but its ties to the denomination should not supersede or interfere with its commitment to, and its relationship with, the Body of Christ within that locality. The greatest challenge to any church is maintaining unity within the larger Body of Christ in the city where you live and serve.

There are many other questions you might ask about house churches. But the most important one is this: "Lord, do you want me to be a part of helping to fulfill the Great Commission by being involved in multiplying house churches in my own country and throughout the world?" There are many ways to plant new churches and thus extend the kingdom of God on the earth. We will accept and not criticize the various ways that God's people are seeking to plant churches.

Summary

It is my firm belief that within the near future, there will be a house church movement in every country on earth. I believe it is the only way we will see the fulfillment of the Great Commission. It is already beginning to happen. God is speaking *The Church in the House* to people everywhere. The ground work has been laid over the past twenty-five years through what has happened worldwide in the broad acceptance of the cell group movement.

Not so long ago it was highly questionable to start a house group of any kind outside the church buildings themselves for fear that it would draw people away from the *church*. Now these groups are seen as very desirable as a means of church growth. But God is calling us to take a further step and recognize that we can actually have a church, in the fullest sense of the word, in a house.

Some of the largest congregations in the world today had their beginning in a house. When did it become a church? Was it a church when it had ten people and met in a house? Or when it had a thousand people and met in a specially designed building called a church? The answer is obvious. It was a church when it began in the house, and if it had continued to meet in a house it would have continued to be a church.

God is stirring and shaking our present church structures and bringing us back to basics. Much of what we now have come to think of as essential is not really essential at all. When we look at the simplicity of the New Testament church and compare it with the institutionalized church of our day we see little, if any, resemblance. The church in some countries looks more like a corporation. Denominational hierarchies, consisting of huge networks that, in many cases, are ruled over along political lines rather than through God-ordained spiritual authority. This has caused immeasurable grief and division for hundreds of years.

May God give us the insight, the humility, and the grace to admit how far we have strayed from the simplicity and the purity of the New Testament church and return to it in brokenness and repentance.

We are excited about multiplying churches in every country and in every group of people so "that repentance and remission of sins will be preached in His name to all nations."

We are finding that a good way to multiply churches is to start Bible colleges. The following is the vision statement for Alpha-Omega Bible Colleges which is a simple and yet very effective method to raise up leaders of simple churches and other Bible colleges. These colleges can function with as few as two or three people who will commit to a one-year course of study that takes them into hands-on, practical training leading both churches and Bible colleges.

Alpha-Omega
Bible College

The definition of the word *college* is "a society of persons joined together for the pursuit of scientific or literary studies." The word itself comes from two Latin words that simply mean "a group of people gathered together." The purpose of Alpha-Omega Bible College is to experience the transforming power of the Bible within the context of a small group of believers gathered to minister to the Lord Jesus and to one another.

The Alpha-Omega Bible College is a one-year, through-the-Bible course. Each student will go through the New Testament in interactive Bible study in class and read through the Old Testament in his/her private devotions at home. The school includes a seminar at the beginning, one evening meeting a week, and a graduation banquet at the end of the school. The vision of ABC is to equip believers in every country in evangelism, discipleship, mercy ministries, and world mission.

Evangelism ABC teaches evangelism on a daily basis in everyday life situations. At each session, time will be given to share experiences in personal evangelism as the Lord opens hearts and sets up "divine appointments" in answer to the following prayer: "Father, cause my path to cross the

path today of someone who is hungry for you. Give me
sensitivity to know when that happens and grace to open my
mouth and share Christ in the power of the Holy Spirit."

Discipleship ABC itself is our method of helping
disciple people in the things of God. The vision is to
multiply these schools into every nation, networking with
other churches, ministries, and missionary organizations.

Mercy Ministries Healing, deliverance, and ministering
in spiritual gifts will be taught in class by hands-on
experience. Projects for helping the poor and needy are part
of the training.

World Mission Each ABC will adopt an unreached
people group for prayer and support in helping to reach that
particular group. We will also network with other
missionary organizations to help in the placement of those
students who are led to serve the Lord in other countries
either short-term or long-term.

Important Information The seminar will cover the first
three sessions of the life of Christ from the book *Jesus Christ,
the Greatest Life Ever Lived* by Johnston Cheney, a unique
blending of all four gospels into one story, leaving nothing
out and repeating nothing.

After the seminar the classes will meet once a week.
They will normally meet in a home and be limited to no more
than fifteen students in order to maintain the small
discussion group dynamic. Each session will include praise,
prayer, sharing, personal ministry, discussion Bible study,
refreshments, and fellowship.

The teaching method will be Interactive Bible Study
which is simply reading and discussing what is read. There
will be a leader or facilitator, but no teacher, as such,
although there will be lots of teaching taking place as the
material is discussed. Questions and comments are
encouraged. We trust the teaching ministry of the Holy
Spirit, along with the insights and balance of the group, to
give light and understanding into the Word of God. The
more outgoing students are encouraged to practice holding
back, and the quiet ones are encouraged to practice speaking
out more.

In Colossians 4:16 Paul says, "After this letter has been read to you, see that it is also read in the church of the Laodiceans and that you in turn read the letter from Laodicea." Paul was confident that the Holy Spirit would enable common, ordinary believers to understand the contents of his letters simply by reading them. This reasoning applies to all Scripture.

We will read and discuss the New Testament in class together, and the homework will be to read through the Old Testament consecutively, reading about two chapters each day. Listening to the Old Testament on cassette tapes or CD is acceptable. No grades will be given. Those who satisfactorily complete the course by attending the retreat, attending the weekly classes, and doing the required reading and outreach projects will receive a Certificate of Completion.

There are two phases of the ABC — the study phase and the outreach phase, and they both take place at the same time. The study phase consists of attending the weekly meetings and reading through the Old Testament. The outreach phase is to pray daily for divine appointments, witness to the lost, minister healing and deliverance to the sick and oppressed during class times and help start a new ABC and/or house church at the end of the course. At the graduation banquet we will announce the time and place of the new ABC and/or house church and invite all who are interested to enroll.

The only cost of the ABC is the book mentioned above. Freewill offerings will be received each week for the school leader in the spirit of Galatians 6:6, "Anyone who receives instruction in the Word must share all good things with his instructor."

Our goal is to see simple Bible colleges and house churches established in every country to help fulfill Jesus' command to go into all the world and proclaim the good news of God's love and forgiveness to all nations.

For more details see contact information on next page.

About the Author

Robert Fitts received Jesus as his personal Savior at the age of eleven in a small tent meeting in Chester, Arkansas. World Missionary Evangelism has been on Robert's heart since he read the lives of David Brainard and Adoniram Judson, pioneer missionaries of early America. He has served in pastoral and missionary evangelism for the past forty years. Since the late seventies he has had an itinerant ministry traveling into other countries with the message of God's love and forgiveness through Jesus Christ.

In 1970 Robert founded Outreach Fellowship, a mission with a vision to train and send outreach teams into other countries to conduct evangelistic crusades and to plant churches. OFI works closely with other missionary organizations such as International Crusades and Radio Evangelism, Youth With A Mission, United States Center for World Mission, and Dawn Ministries in order to fulfill the Great Commission.

Robert and his wife Joni live in Kona, Hawaii, where they work with the University of the Nations, a ministry of Youth With A Mission, as well as with the local churches on the Big Island when they are not traveling. They have seven children and sixteen grandchildren.

The message God has given them to share with the Body of Christ is salvation, healing, deliverance, simple church, simple Bible college, and the central message of "Christ in you, the hope of glory."

Robert Fitts Ministries
76-6309 Haku Place
Kailua-Kona, HI 96740
Phone: 1-808-334-9682
Fax: 1-808-334-9673
e-mail: RobertJoni@aol.com

Bibliography

Allen, Roland. *Missionary Methods: St. Paul's or Ours.* Chicago: Moody Press, 1956.

Atkerson, Steve, ed. *Toward a House Church Theology.* New Testament Restoration Foundation, 2752 Evans Dale Circle, Atlanta, GA 30340, 1996.

Banks, Robert. *Going to Church in the First Century.* The SeedSowers Publishing, P.O. Box 285, Sargent, GA 30275, 1980.

Banks, Robert. *Paul's Idea of Community.* Grand Rapids: Eerdmans, 1979.

Banks, Robert and Julia. *The Church Comes Home.* Peabody, MS: Hendrickson Publishers, 1998.

Broadbent, E.H. *The Pilgrim Church.* London: Pickering and Inglis, Ltd., 1931.

Brunner, Emil. *The Misunderstanding of the Church.* London: Utterworth Press, 1952.

Clark, Steve. *Patterns of Christian Community.* Servant Books, P.O. Box 8617, Ann Arbor, MI 48107.

Coleman, Robert E. *The Master Plan of Evangelism.* Tappan, N.J.: Fleming H. Revell, 1963.

Ellison, H.L. *Household Church.* Paternoster Press, 1963.

Girard, Robert C. *Brethren Hang Loose.* Grand Rapids: Zondervan, 1972.

Gunderson, Denny. *The Leadership Paradox.* YWAM Publishing, Seattle.

Hadway, Dubose and Wright. *Home Cell Groups and House Churches.* Nashville: Broadman Press, 1987.

Hay, Alexander. *New Testament Order.* Audubon, N.J.: New Testament Missionary Union, 1947.

Kreider, Larry. *House to House: Spiritual Insights for the 21st Century Church.* Touch Outreach Ministries, P.O. Box 19888, Houston, TX 77079, 1995.

Krupp, Nate. *God's Simple Plan for His Church.* Salem, OR: Preparing the Way Publishers, 1993.

Krupp, Nate. *New Wine Skins.* Salem, OR: Preparing the Way Publishers, 1990.

Krupp, Nate. *The Church Triumphant at the End of the Age.* Destiny Image Publishers, P.O. Box 351, Shippensburg, PA 17257, 1993.

Kung, Hans. *Church.* Sheed & Ward Publishers, 1976.

Kurosaki, Kokichi. *One Body in Christ.* Northridge, CA: Voice Christian Publications. 1968.

Montgomery, Jim. *Dawn – 2000; Seven Million Churches to Go.* William Carey Library, P.O. Box 40129, Pasadena, CA 98114, 1996.

Nee, Watchman. *The Church and the Work.* Richmond, VA: Christian Fellowship Publishers, 1982.

Nee, Watchman. *The Normal Christian Church Life.* Living Stream Ministry, P.O. Box 2121, Anaheim, CA 92804, 1980.

Neighbour, Ralph W. *Where Do We Go from Here? A Guidebook for Cell Group Churches.* Touch Publications, P.O. Box 19888, Houston, TX 77224, 1990.

Ogden, Greg. *The New Reformation.* Grand Rapids: Zondervan, 1990.

Paul, Steven R. *Liberating the Laity.* Downer's Grove, IL: Inter-Varsity Press, 1985.

Peters, Mike. *Meetings in His Kingdom: Jesus Personally Leading His Church . . . in Home, City, and Multi-City Gatherings.* Kingdom Publishing, P.O. Box 68309, Indianapolis, IN 46268, 1990.

Petersen, Jim. *Church Without Walls: Moving Beyond Traditional Boundaries.* Colorado Springs, CO: NavPress, 1992.

Pethybridge, W.J. *A Lost Secret of the Early Church.* Minneapolis, MN: Bethany Publishers.

Rinehart, Stacy. *The Paradox of Servant Leadership.* Colorado Springs, CO: NavPress.

Rutz, James. *1700 Years is Long Enough.* The SeedSowers, P.O. Box 285, Sargent, GA, 1991.

Rutz, James. *The Open Church.* The SeedSowers, P.O. Box 285, Sargent, GA, 1992.

Simson, Wolfgang. *Houses that Change the World.* Available on the internet at 100337.2106@compuserve.com.

Smith, Christian. *Going to the Root: Nine Proposals for Radical Church Renewal.* Scottdale, PA: Herald Press, 1992.

Snyder, Graydon. *Church Life Before Constantine.* SeedSowers Publishing, P.O. Box 285, Sargent, GA 30275, 1985.

Snyder, Howard. *Community of the King.* Downer's Grove, IL: Inter-Varsity Press, 1978.

Snyder, Howard. *Liberating the Church.* Downer's Grove, IL: Inter-Varsity Press, 1975.

Snyder, Howard. *The Problem of Wineskins.* Downer's Grove, IL: Inter-Varsity Press, 1975.

Snyder, Howard. *The Radical Wesley and Patterns for Church Renewal.* Downer's Grove, IL: Inter-Varsity Press, 1980.

Stedman, Ray C. *Body Life.* Regal Books, 2300 Knoll Dr., Ventura, CA 93003, 1972.

Strauch, Alexander. *Biblical Eldership.* Lewis and Roth Publishers, P.O. Box 569, Littleton, CO 80160, 1988.

Viola, Frank. *Rethinking the Wineskin: The Practice of the New Testament Church.* SeedSowers Publishing, P.O. Box 285, Sargent, GA 30275.

Viola, Frank. *Who is Your Covering? A Fresh Look at Leadership, Authority and Accountability.* SeedSowers Publishing, P.O. Box 285, Sargent, GA 30275.

Other Books
by Bob Fitts

The Baptism in the Holy Spirit
What it is, how to receive it, and what it does
for you.

Your Faith Will Heal You
Three amazing examples of how building
your faith in the promises of God will bring
healing to your body.

The Revival of Joy
One man's experience of the present day
outpouring of the Holy Spirit.

The Value of Speaking in Tongues
Moving into a deeper level of prayer, praise,
intercession, and spiritual warfare through
praying in the Spirit.

Three-Step Prayer for Guidance
How to hear the voice of God.

Prayer
A strategy for success.

Prosperity through Generosity
A look at the promises of God to bless and
prosper those who give generously.

To order any or all of the above titles, contact Robert Fitts at:
76-6309 Haku Place, Kona, HI 96740
Phone: (808)334-9682
FAX: (808)334-9673
email: <Robertjoni@aol.com>
Note: These messages are sent out on a free-will offering basis as the
Lord provides the funds for printing and postage.

Additional Books from PTWP
that will help you discover
God's Plan for His Church

God's Simple Plan for His Church – by Nate Krupp
A radical look at God's biblical plan for His Church.
How the Great Commission can be fulfilled very quickly
by a multiplication of simple house-churches.
ISBN 1-929451-12-1, 175 pages, $11.95

The Church Triumphant at the End of the Age – by
Nate Krupp. The end-time Church characterized by
revival, restoration, unity, world evangelization, and
persecution. Also traces revival, restoration, and world
evangelization throughout Church history. A major
work.   360 pages, $12.95

New Wine Skins – the Church in Transition – by Nate
Krupp. Fifteen ways that God is changing His Church
today to get ready for coming end-time revival, harvest,
and persecution.   ISBN 1-929451-14-8, 22 pages, $5

Leadership-Servanthood in the Church – by Nate
Krupp. A book which examines every major passage in
the New Testament on the subject of leadership. You
may be surprised at some of the findings.
ISBN 1-929451-15-6, 22 pages, $4

WOMAN – God's Plan, not Man's Tradition – by
Joanne Krupp. This book examines every major
passage in the Bible on the subject of God's plan for
women. It refutes the traditional teaching of husbands
having authority over their wives and of a limited role
for women in the Church. It biblically releases women to
become all that God intends them to be as equal partners
in the home and the Church.
ISBN 1-929451-00-8, 154 pages, $10.95

Restoring the Vision of the End-times Church – by Vern
Kuenzi. This is not a typical book on how to improve the
church. This is a very strong word to the Body of Christ
on what's ahead for God's people. As a theological-
biblical treatise it is the best exposition seen on the
subject of the Church and end-times. But it is more than
that. It is a major prophetic word to the Church about
her future.   ISBN 1-929451-01-6, 252 pages, $14.95

ORDER FORM

Preparing the Way Publishing

2121 Barnes Avenue SE, Salem, OR 97306, USA

Voice 503-585-4054 • Fax 503-375-8401

E-mail: kruppnj@open.org • Website: www.PTWpublish.com

Books About the Church

QTY	TITLE	PRICE	TOTAL
_____	God's Simple Plan for His Church	$11.95	_____
_____	The Church Triumphant	$12.95	_____
_____	New Wine Skins – the Church in Transition	$5.00	_____
_____	Leadership-Servanthood in the Church	$4.00	_____
_____	Woman – God's Plan not Man's Tradition	$10.95	_____
_____	Restoring the Vision of the End-times Church .	$14.95	_____

Ordering Information:

Fill in your order and send it **with payment** to Preparing the Way Publishers for processing. A new copy of this Order Form will be included with your order for your future ordering use.

Payments:

To avoid extra bookkeeping and handling expenses, credits for less than $1.00 will not be sent. Prices are subject to change without notice. **Full payment is expected with order.**

Postage and Handling:

For mainland United States orders:

Amount of Order	P & H
Under $20.00	$3.00
$20.00 - $39.99	15%
$40.00 and above	10%

For Alaska, Hawaii, U.S. possessions, and all other nations:

Actual postage charge plus 10% handling

TOTAL Book Order $ _____

Postage & Handling $ _____

GRAND TOTAL $ _____

Ship To:

Name: _____   Date of Order: _____

Address: _____

City _____   State _____   Zip _____

Nation: _____   Telephone: _____

Printed in the United States
932900001B